MOUNTAIN MEN
OF THE
AMERICAN WEST

MOUNTAIN MEN
OF THE
AMERICAN WEST

by

James A.
Crutchfield

tamarack books inc

First Edition, Trade: May, 1997
10 9 8 7 6 5 4 3 2 1

ISBN 1–886609–07–1

The cover is an original painting,
"No Time to Linger," by H. David Wright.
Prints and more information about the paintings of
H. David Wright are available from
Grey Stone Press, 205 Louise Avenue, Nashville, TN 37203,
1–800–251–2664.

Interior original artwork by author.

Published by:
Tamarack Books, Inc.
PO Box 190313
Boise, ID 83719-0313
1-800-962-6657

Printed in the United States of America

TABLE OF CONTENTS

THE BOOK YOU ARE ABOUT TO READ is an effort to bring together a variety of reference material that deals with the western American fur trade period. That romantic phase of our national history lasted roughly from about 1806, when Lewis and Clark returned to St. Louis from their journey to the Pacific Ocean, until the late 1840s, when immigrants along the Oregon and California Trails rapidly replaced the mountain man as the spearhead of westward movement across the continent.

Within the last fifty years, scores of books have been written that depict the life and times of the mountain men and the rigorous life they led in search of wealth and adventure in the vast reaches of the American West. Biographies of individual players in this drama have been published, as well as more general works that document the operations of the major fur companies and the impact they and their employees made on the exploration and eventual settlement of the trans-Mississippi River region. Indeed, there is no shortage of good, readable, accurate books about America's western fur trade.

What I wanted to accomplish with the present volume, however—and I hope I have achieved my objective—

was to provide the reader with enough basic data about the period and to whet his appetite enough that he would follow up on his interest and continue his research in greater depth. In order to accomplish this mission, I have divided the book into three major parts. The first section presents a brief, yet I believe, satisfactory, historical overview of the western fur trade period. Part II consists of thumbnail biographies of nearly one hundred mountain men and associated shakers and movers in the fur trade. A comprehensive bibliography of books that deal with all facets of the western fur trade comprises Part III.

A reference book such as this one relies heavily on the works of other writers. Most, if not all, of the existing material that I referred to is listed in Part III. My thanks go to the many historians and writers, past and present, who had the foresight to document this important phase of history and to preserve it, through the written word, for future generations of readers.

I would especially like to thank the Idaho Historical Society for some of the photographs used in this volume. Although contemporary word pictures and verbal descriptions of yesteryear's mountain men legends are interesting and they fill a great void in our understanding of the past when visual material is not available, it is even more exciting to look upon graphic images of these people and to see their countenances just as their associates did.

PART ONE

A BRIEF HISTORY

THE NORTH AMERICAN FUR TRADE, of which the western theater was only one part, had its beginnings when the first European explorer set foot on the shores of the North Atlantic. Furs were already an important item of commerce in Europe, and it was only natural that seafarers from Scandinavia—and later, from France, England, and Spain—took a hard look at the New World for the presence of animals that could add profit to adventure. From that long-ago day around 1,000 A.D. when Indians along the northeast coast of America offered to trade to the Vikings "packs wherein were grey furs, sables, and all kind of peltries," the contest for ascendancy in the American fur business was on.

The French, who later became the major European player in the battle for North American fur, were the first to discover that huge profits could be made by swapping simple items of trade to the Indians who lived along the St. Lawrence River. The wonderful goods that French traders had to offer the Indians in exchange for their furs—iron ware, beads, fishhooks, knives, hatchets, and colored cloth—were just too overwhelming for the natives. "They gave us whatsoever they had, not keeping anything, so that they were constrained to go backe againe naked, and made us signes that the next day they would come againe, and bring more skinnes with them," exclaimed a bewildered Jacques Cartier after a trading mission near the mouth of the St. Lawrence in the 1530s.

English explorers and settlers found present-day North Carolina and Virginia to be just as rich in fur—and populated with Indians willing to trade them—as the northeast coastal areas frequented by the French. As early as 1588, Thomas Hariot, a young surveyor and historian who had been sent to the New World three years earlier by Sir Walter Raleigh, proclaimed that:

> All along the seacoast there are many otters, and if they could be caught by weirs and other traps, they would make us good profits. We hope also to get marten furs, for the people say that in some places they are plentiful. . . .

Twenty years later, Hariot's countryman, John Smith, also wrote from Virginia that the countryside abounded with "Wilde Cats . . . Martins, Powlcats, weessels and Minkes. . . . Otters, Beavers, Martins, Luswarts and sables."

In 1670, King Charles II of England signed the "Charter of the Governor and Company of Adventurers," thus launching the Hudson's Bay Company. Hudson's Bay quickly became the largest fur company in North America, and in time extended its influence throughout Canada and, later, into the American Pacific Northwest.

Although Spanish explorers were more interested in exploiting their sphere of influence for its gold and silver content, they, too, carried on trade with the Indians for furs, hides, and peltries. By 1580, deerskins were already an object of great value to Spanish colonists in St. Augustine, and by the seventeenth century, they were being used as currency in other parts of Spanish Florida. In the far southwest, early Spanish conquistadors commented on the bisonhide trading system among the Plains tribes and the village-dwelling Pueblos. Later, when Hispanic towns and villages began to spring up in the region, the settlers participated in a more extensive hide and fur trade with the natives.

By the time the infant United States began to flex its muscles, European exploitation of the fur trade in the extreme eastern part of the continent was rapidly coming to an end, primarily because the major fur-bearing mammals had been extirpated from the region. In 1777, a young British army officer named Thomas Anburey thoughtfully commented on the demise of the eastern Canadian beaver population when he wrote:

> It was no sooner understood that Canada was stored with Beavers, than the savages . . . directed their war against an animal the most harmless, who molests no living creature, and is neither carniverous nor sanguinary . . . a circumstance entirely owing to the unmerciful rapaciousness which luxury had made neces-

3

sary in skins, for all the polished nations of Europe.

Anburey's concern about the greedy assault and subsequent virtual extinction of eastern Canada's beaver population could, likewise, have been directed to that part of the United States that lay between the Atlantic Ocean and the Appalachian Mountains.

In 1796, the United States Congress attempted to get a handle on the fur industry west of the Appalachian Mountains by passing legislation that called for the permanent establishment of "factories," or government-owned trading posts, to be used in the Indian trade. Dealings in furs were strictly regulated by the government, and the organization of the factory system left no place for private citizens to engage in any aspect of the business. Under the scheme, quality trade goods were warehoused at the various factories and used to barter with the neighboring Indians who were persuaded to bring their furs to such posts for exchange.

In order to implement the factory system, an appropriation of $150,000 was made to add more factories to the two that were opened in Tennessee and Georgia the previous year. By 1805, several factories were operating east of the Mississippi, along with three situated west of the stream: Fort Bellefontaine, at the mouth of the Missouri River; Arkansas Post, at the mouth of the Arkansas River, and at Natchitoches, in lower Louisiana.

While the federal government was attempting to regulate the fur trade in the East through the implementation and administration of the factory system, French, English, and Spanish agents still pretty much held control over the fur business in the trans-Mississippi West.

In 1794, the Missouri Company, more formally known as "La Campagnie de Commerce pour la Decouverte des Nations du haut du Missouri," was organized at St. Louis to explore and trade with Missouri River tribes that lived in the vast Spanish-controlled Louisiana Territory. Among the company's principals were noted fur-men Pierre and Auguste Chouteau, Jean Papin, Joseph Ribidoux, and Jacques Clamorgan. Less than one month after these French entrepreneurs had filed their organization papers, Jean Baptiste Truteau and eight companions left St. Louis on the company's first trading mission among the middle Missouri River tribes.

In 1795, James MacKay, a Scots fur trader who had recently changed his citizenship from Great Britain to Spain, joined the company and traveled up the Missouri River, his mission to "open commerce with those distant and Unknown Nations in the upper parts of his Catholic Majesty's Dominions through that continent as far as the Pacific Ocean." Two years later, David Thompson, an English trader, visited the Mandans on the upper Missouri in an unsuccessful attempt to persuade the Indians to switch their allegiance from the Missouri Company to the Canadian-controlled North West Company.

The fact that all of this foreign commerce was taking place on land that he thought should rightfully belong to the United States deeply troubled President Thomas Jefferson. For years, he had dreamed of an American empire that stretched all the way to the Pacific Ocean. But, every time he attempted to organize a mission to explore the vast wilderness expanses of the Far West, his plans were thwarted.

Jefferson's first attempt to realize his westward-looking aspirations occurred in 1783, when he was a forty-year old congressman from Virginia. He approached George Rogers Clark about his far-reaching idea to explore the trans-Mississippi region, but nothing came of his premature plans. Nine years later, when the American sea captain, Robert Gray of Boston, discovered the mouth of the Columbia River, Jefferson—now secretary of state in President George Washington's cabinet—again set the wheels in motion.

This time, Jefferson approached Andre Michaux, a renowned French naturalist who was visiting the United States on a research mission. With the support and financial backing of the American Philosophical Society, Jefferson hired Michaux to "explore the country along the Missouri" and "to find the shortest & most convenient route of communication between the U.S. & the Pacific ocean . . . & to learn such particulars as can be obtained of the country through which it passes, it's productions, inhabitants & other interesting circumstances." Before Michaux got fully underway on his mission, he was recalled to France and Thomas Jefferson's dreams were once again smashed.

In 1803, when Jefferson as president of the United States got the chance to purchase Louisiana from war-torn France for fifteen million dollars, he jumped at the opportunity. Even before the papers were signed transferring the 828,000 square miles of Louisiana to American ownership, Jefferson had convinced Congress to appropriate a sum of money to finance an expedition to the Pacific. For the leader of this mission, the President chose his former personal secretary and close family friend, Meriwether Lewis. Lewis selected his one-time army associate and comrade, William Clark, as his co-commander.

It is not the purpose of this introductory overview of the western fur trade to explore the logistics and final results of the Lewis and Clark Expedition. It is important to remember, however, that the majority of the territory that lay west of the Mississippi River was largely unknown to Americans when the two captains began their "voyage of discovery" up the Missouri River from St. Louis in May, 1804. Charged by President Jefferson to explore and map the vast western wilderness and to bring home descriptions—and specimens, if possible—of the various wildlife and other natural phenomena along the way, Lewis, Clark, and the men of the Expedition accomplished their mission to near perfection.

Lewis and Clark found an abundance of beaver. Beginning in the vicinity of today's Platte County, Missouri, all the way to the Pacific, Expedition members observed huge populations of the furry rodent. The journals kept by the two captains, as well as those written by Patrick Gass, John Ordway, and Charles Floyd, contain scores of entries describing the beaver in his natural habitat and marveling at his seemingly endless numbers.

By now, in the territory east of the Mississippi River, the fur trade was practically a thing of the past. The two hundred years and more of primarily French—but in later times, American as well—trapping and trading with eastern Indian tribes for precious beaver pelts had driven the rodent to virtual extinction in the entire region that stretched from the Gulf of Mexico to the Great Lakes and from the Atlantic Ocean to the banks of the Mississippi.

But, the extirpation of the beaver in the original thirteen colonies and their western extensions did little to decrease the demand for the animal's valuable pelt in the large American cities, England, and on the Continent. The beaver fur hat, an article of high fashion that had been popular in Europe for three hundred years, was the culprit behind the small animal's demise, both abroad and in the eastern United States. Hat manufacturers believed that just because the critters had become extinct in the East was no reason why the vast wilderness areas of the Far West should not be exploited.

When news of their immense numbers became known in the East from published accounts of the Lewis and Clark Expedition, the beaver's future along the Missouri River, in the Rocky Mountains, and in other parts of the American West was sealed. A sign of the times to come was revealed by William Clark, when he wrote—in his usual less-than-perfect English—the following in his journal on August 22, 1806:

> . . . the Cheifs of the Chyennes lodge he requested me to Send Some traders to them, that their country was full of beaver and they would then be encouraged to Kill beaver, but now they had no use for them as they could get nothing for their skins and did not know well, how to catch beaver. If the white people would come amongst them they would become acquainted with them and the white people would learn them how to take the beaver. I promised the Nation that I

would inform their Great father the President of
the U States, and he would have them Supplied
with goods. . . .

     In the late summer of 1806, when Lewis and Clark
were on the final leg of their return trip from the Pacific
Ocean to St. Louis, they were met by two trappers named
Forrest Hancock and Joseph Dickson. Rumors had already
begun to circulate back East about the large numbers of
beaver and other fur-bearing animals that Expedition
members had found on their westward journey. The two
men were traveling to the Rocky Mountains to capitalize
on the abundance of beaver there. But, they were unfamiliar with the territory and prevailed upon John Colter, one
of the Expedition's best men, to guide them. Colter con-
sulted with his commanders, and they agreed to release
him from Expedition service. Colter's return to the mountains that summer marked the beginning of America's leap
into the western fur trade.

     Although it lasted for less than forty years—and, to
use an old saying of the times, was merely a "flash in the
pan" in the five hundred-year-old saga of America—the
western fur trade era was one of the most important periods in United States history. During the few years between
the return of Lewis and Clark in the summer of 1806, and
the day in 1843 when grizzled old Jim Bridger threw open
the gates of his newly constructed fort in present-day western Wyoming, the western fur trade began, reached its climax, and died.

◆ ◆ ◆

Forrest Hancock and Joseph Dickson had just van-
ished into the wilderness of the Rocky Mountains, and
Lewis and Clark had only recently returned to St. Louis to
a hero's welcome, when a Louisiana-born, St. Louis-based
Spaniard named Manuel Lisa decided to try his hand at
the new western fur trade. In 1807, Lisa took a small detail
of trader/trappers up the Missouri River as far as the confluence of the Bighorn and Yellowstone Rivers, where his
men quickly built Fort Lisa, or Manuel's Fort as it is sometimes called.

Lisa returned to St. Louis, and in 1809, he organized
the St. Louis Missouri Fur Company, more commonly
known as the Missouri Fur Company. For the next couple
of years, Lisa sent his outfit's expeditions up its namesake
stream, and his coffers alternated between full and empty
as the company vigorously pursued its business. A post
was established in the Three Forks area, and another one
was built across the Continental Divide on the Snake
River. But by 1811, when all three of the company's fur
posts were abandoned because of the futility in trying to
deal with the hostile Blackfeet tribe, Lisa shifted his center of operations back downstream and established new
headquarters at Council Bluffs.

Over the years, the Missouri Fur Company experi-
enced a number of reorganizations, until finally, in 1819,
Lisa was appointed its president. He was the only one of
the original founders to remain active with the company.
His crowning success was short-lived, however, for in
August, 1820, the entrepreneur died.

Upon the death of Lisa, his associate, Joshua Pilcher,
took over the day-to-day operations of Missouri Fur. One of
Pilcher's first acts was to reopen the upriver trade, and in

the fall of 1821, upon the site of the old Fort Lisa, he built a new structure which he called Fort Benton. Under Pilcher's management, the company soared to financial success, and the following year, more than twenty thousand dollars worth of furs were shipped downriver to St. Louis. With three hundred men in the field, Missouri Fur was finally on its way to the success that had so often eluded its founder.

But then, the Blackfeet menace resurfaced. In the spring of 1823, Pilcher sent two traders, Robert Jones and Michael Immel, along with twenty-eight companions, into the Three Forks region of the upper Missouri River, again hoping to establish peaceful contact with members of the Blackfeet tribe. Pilcher instructed Jones and Immel to "use every effort to obtain a friendly interview with the Blackfoot Indians, and to incur any reasonable expense for the accomplishment of that object; and to impress them with the friendly disposition of American citizens towards them. . . ."

In May, Jones and Immel encountered a party of Blackfeet warriors along Jefferson's Fork of the Missouri. In what initially appeared to be a friendly meeting, the two groups exchanged pleasantries, and the Indians warmed to the idea that trading houses might be established in the region. On the following morning, the Blackfeet left in a peaceable mood.

Jones, Immel, and their trappers immediately left the area, anxious to get home with their cargo of valuable furs. When they arrived in the vicinity of present-day Billings, Montana, four hundred screaming Blackfeet burst out of the rimrock, and in a matter of minutes, Jones, Immel, and five of their followers were killed. The Indians took all of the traders' property, including thirty-five packs of beaver plews and several horses and traps, all amounting to about sixteen thousand dollars in value.

The final blow had been delivered to the Missouri Fur Company. When he received word of the disaster, a devastated Joshua Pilcher wrote,

> This our second adventure to the mountains, had surpassed my most sanguine expectations; success was complete and my views were fulfilled in every respect. . . . The flower of my business is gone; my mountaineers have been defeated, and the chiefs of the party both slain.

Manuel Lisa's Missouri Fur Company dominated the Missouri River fur trade for a decade and more. But while the St. Louis-based outfit wielded its influence over the Great Plains and eastern front of the Rocky Mountains, another company had established itself at the mouth of the Columbia River and made serious inroads into the wilderness from the west.

In the spring of 1811, at about the same time Manuel Lisa was focusing his Missouri Fur Company's operations along the middle Missouri River, sixteen men made their way through the damp undergrowth of thick evergreen forest overlooking the Columbia River and began work on a stockaded fur post that they called Astoria. Named after John Jacob Astor, the founder of the American Fur Company and its subsidiary, the Pacific Fur Company, the fort was intended to provide a home base for Astor's traders and trappers from which they could combat the powerful North West Company, owned and operated by Canadians.

Astor's scheme to develop his far-reaching fur empire was to send two separate parties, one by land and the other by sea, to the mouth of the Columbia, where the center for his Pacific operations would be built. The overland party left Montreal in July, 1810, under the leadership of Wilson Price Hunt and Donald McKenzie. The ocean-bound group, aboard the ship, *Tonquin,* set sail from New York two months earlier. The ship's party arrived at the Columbia first, and its crew immediately began work on Astoria.

Astor's dreams of dominating the western fur business were no more successful than Manuel Lisa's. By mid-1812, the United States and Great Britain were once again at war, and in October of the following year, operatives of the North West Company, Astor's arch-rival along the Columbia, marched on Astoria and occupied the post. All of the furs, furnishings, and supplies were commandeered in exchange for a cash settlement worth only about one-third of the fort's actual value. In December the British formally occupied Astoria and changed its name to Fort George. Now, after only two and a half years in the business, Astor's influence on the western fur trade was placed on hold, and he was temporarily relegated to his earlier fur interests around the Great Lakes. It would be almost a decade before his dominance would again be felt in the trans-Mississippi River West.

It was not only the upper Missouri River basin and the Pacific Northwest that held the interest of the American fur trading and trapping community. Manuel Lisa developed an early interest in trading with citizens of Santa Fe, but after several unsuccessful attempts, he returned to his Missouri River endeavors. By the second decade of the nineteenth century, other St. Louis-based fur traders were frequenting New Mexico and the southern Rocky Mountains region. Ezekiel Williams and several other Americans trapped the upper Arkansas River valley beginning in 1811. In the fall of 1815, Auguste P. Chouteau and Jules DeMun obtained licenses permitting them to trade and trap among the Arapaho Indians who lived around the headwaters of the Arkansas River. Two years later, Spanish officials arrested both men, hauled them off to Santa Fe, confiscated their furs and trade goods worth thirty thousand dollars, and imprisoned them for forty-eight days.

In 1821, Mexico won its independence from Spain. Anxious to improve its commercial relations with the United States, Mexican officials opened their streams and rivers to American trappers. During that year and the next, Jacob Fowler, Hugh Glenn, and eighteen other trapper/traders journeyed to the headwaters of the Arkansas, where they explored and trapped the region for several weeks.

In addition to Mexico attaining its independence in 1821, the year was a momentous one for the western American fur trade on other fronts. In March, the giant British-controlled Hudson's Bay Company and its Canadian competitor, the North West Company, merged operations. The resulting establishment, still called the

Hudson's Bay Company, was termed by one historian as "an enterprise of power unequaled in the history of the fur trade." Five days later, the United States Congress passed a bill that abolished the government-controlled factory system, thereby opening the doors to the lucrative American fur trade with the Indians to any and all comers. The legislation was engineered by the Missouri senator, Thomas Hart Benton, at the urging of American Fur Company officials, including John Jacob Astor and his field lieutenant Ramsey Crooks, who by now had their sights set on a re-entry into the Missouri River trade.

In 1822, another outfit was formed that had a tremendous effect on the western trade. Although by now, the fur industry had become a business that accommodated both traders and trappers who worked for the same company, this new organization was about to change that relationship. The days of traders swapping trinkets to Indians for their furs—the procedure that had been followed in the East and around the Great Lakes for scores of years—were about gone. The era of the highly individualistic trapper, the fabled "mountain man," who lived off the land and trapped his own pelts, was about to begin.

On February 13, 1822, the *Missouri Gazette & Public Advertiser* carried a notice within its pages that marked the beginning of this fascinating period in American history. The advertisement read:

The Subscriber wishes to engage ONE HUN-
DRED MEN, to ascend the river Missouri to its
source, there to be employed for one, two, or
three years—For particulars, enquire of Major
Andrew Henry, near the Lead Mines, in the
County of Washington, (who will ascend with,
and command the party) or to the subscriber at
St. Louis.

William Ashley

Several days later, the *St. Louis Enquirer* carried
Ashley's announcement, and for the next few weeks, the
notice appeared in other Missouri newspapers as well. The
far-ranging Rocky Mountain Fur Company, although not
called by that name until sometime later, had its beginnings from the date of that advertisement. Before it, too,
passed out of existence years later, the company would
have on its payroll—in addition to General Ashley and
Major Henry—many of the legends of the fur trade, including Jedediah Smith, Jim Bridger, David E. Jackson,
William and Milton Sublette, Etienne Provost, Robert
Campbell, Thomas Fitzpatrick, Jim Beckwourth, Edward
Rose, Mike Fink, Moses Harris, and Hugh Glass, among
others.

As successful as the Ashley-Henry firm eventually
became, it, too, had its share of trouble during the early
days. Although Henry established a strong presence at the
confluence of the Yellowstone and Missouri Rivers during
the fall of 1822, the company lost ten thousand dollars
worth of trade goods that year when one of its boats was
destroyed by the rapid currents of the fickle Missouri.

Then, an additional setback was experienced the following year when Ashley started upriver to resupply Henry's trappers who had wintered on the Yellowstone. When the general reached the Arikara villages, located atop the steep west bank of the Missouri River in present-day South Dakota, the Indians attacked his two boat loads of men and supplies and forced them back downriver. After Ashley's traders fought an indecisive battle—reinforced by elements of the Sixth U.S. Infantry regiment under the command of Colonel Henry Leavenworth, along with employees from Joshua Pilcher's Missouri Fur Company— the season was late and Ashley again suffered a large financial loss to his company.

After the Arikara campaign of 1823, Ashley dispatched two trapping parties to the field, one under the leadership of Andrew Henry and the other commanded by Jedediah Smith. During the winter of 1823–24, the two groups trapped in the region beyond the Rockies and found an abundance of beaver there. When they delivered their furs back to the Missouri settlements during the summer of 1824, they informed Ashley of this fact plus the news that they had discovered a way through the mountains that could be negotiated with wagons. The idea that wheeled vehicles could be used for transporting goods and supplies to the mountains, plus the revelation that the Missouri Fur Company was redoubling its efforts to dominate the Missouri River trade, convinced Ashley that his future in the business lay on the far side of the Rockies.

Considering all of the recent developments in the trade, Ashley contemplated a method whereby he could resupply his men in the new area of operations beyond the Rockies by a more direct route. His solution to the dilemma, known ever since as the rendezvous system, revolutionized the entire western fur trade. The premise was actually very simple. Instead of maintaining distant fur posts at various sites in the mountains, Ashley employees would purchase supplies, traps, weapons, liquor, and trade goods in St. Louis and the Missouri settlements and then haul them overland to a pre-selected rendezvous site somewhere in the Rocky Mountains. There, during the warm days of summer, the trappers would descend out of the mountains, spend a week or two with the Ashley resuppliers, swap their furs for the supplies and trade goods they needed, and be off again in time for the fall hunt.

Hiram M. Chittenden, in his classic study, *The American Fur Trade of the Far West,* provides the following colorful description of a typical rendezvous:

> Hither from all directions came the roving population of the surrounding country. First there were the bands of trappers who were in the regular employ of the companies, and who had passed a long and lonesome winter among the mountains. Then there were the freemen, who gathered with the rest to dispose of the fruits of their labors. To the same spot came numerous bands of Indians also with furs or horses to sell.
>
> As soon as everyone expected had arrived, the business began. The parties belonging to the company turned over their furs, and received their wages and a new equipment. The free trappers and the Indians trafficked their furs on the best attainable terms, and purchased their equipments for the ensuing year. While all this

business was going on, and while the cargoes were being made ready for the homeward journey, the heterogeneous assemblage went in for a good time. . . . The caravan then returned to the States, and the . . . trappers . . . betook themselves with heavy hearts but light pockets to their lonely retreats in the mountains, there to spend another three hundred and sixty-five days in peril and toil. . . .

The mountain rendezvous was a remarkable gathering entirely unique in American history.

The benefits of the rendezvous were mutual. Operating this type of resupply system allowed Ashley to obtain the best quality beaver pelts at the point of origin, rather than forcing him to compete with other fur merchants, all of whom were simultaneously trying to convince the Indians to bring them their best furs. The rendezvous allowed the trappers to acquire badly needed supplies and equipment in their home territory, thus saving them hundreds of miles of travel to and from the Missouri settlements. And, from a social standpoint, the rendezvous provided the opportunity for trappers to leave their lonely vigil in the remote mountains and to relax, drink, gamble, and womanize with the Indian maidens who frequented the gatherings with other members of their tribes.

Ashley's first rendezvous took place during the summer of 1825, and, although the general soon left the fur business altogether, the system continued to work for company owner and fur trapper alike. A total of fifteen annual rendezvous were held between 1825 and 1840, the only

Painting of Bear Lake
Credit: Idaho State Historical Society, #83-14.1.

exception being the year 1831 when there was no gathering due to failure of the supply train to reach the rendezvous site on time. The majority of the fifteen took place in the western part of present-day Wyoming, although two of them occurred in eastern Idaho, and four were held in northern Utah.

William Ashley's participation in his rendezvous scheme lasted only two years. After the 1826 gathering, he sold his fledgling fur company (Andrew Henry had already retired and Ashley had taken Jedediah Smith on as a partner for a brief time) to Smith and two other former employees, David Jackson and William Sublette. The new firm, now called Smith Jackson & Sublette, was purchased by the three men for perhaps as much as thirty thousand dollars; the records of the transaction have been lost. The sum was payable to Ashley in beaver furs valued at three dollars per pound. It was an emotional time for Ashley and his men. According to one of them, Jim Beckwourth, Ashley addressed his employees as follows:

> Mountaineers and friends! When I first came to the mountains, I came a poor man. You, by your indefatigable exertions, toils, and privations have procured me an independent fortune. With ordinary prudence in the management of what I have accumulated, I shall never want for any thing. For this, my friends, I feel myself under great obligations to you. . . .

> My friends! I am now about to leave you, to take up my abode in St. Louis. Whenever any of you return thither, your first duty must be to call at my house, to talk over the scenes of peril we have encountered, and partake of the best cheer my table can afford you.

> I now wash my hands of the toils of the Rocky Mountains. Farewell, mountaineers and friends! May God bless you all!

Although he was now out of the day-to-day management of the fur company he had founded, General Ashley, nevertheless, agreed to "furnish said Smith Jackson & Sublette with Merchandise," and promised "That he will furnish no other company or Individual with Merchandise other than those who may be in his immediate service."

As soon as Ashley returned to St. Louis, however, he attempted to enter into a business relationship with another fur outfit, his old competitor, Bernard Pratt & Company. Ashley's offer was to allow Pratt one-half interest in a new enterprise to be called William Ashley & Company, thereby allowing Ashley to circumvent his earlier commitment to Smith, *et al* not to furnish supplies to other companies. Apparently, Ashley's plan was to place more trapping parties into the field, thus going into direct competition not only with his old company, but with himself as supplier to that company as well. As affairs turned out, the partnership was not consummated, since Pratt instead sold out to Astor's American Fur Company, becoming its Western Department.

In the meantime, and for the next four years, the three new partners in Ashley's old company went far afield in the Rocky Mountain wilderness, trapping furiously to maintain their competitive edge over the growing number of other outfits who put their own men into the mountains. Jed Smith made two trips to California during this time. On the last journey, after Umpqua Indians massacred many of his party in southern Oregon, he ended up at Fort Vancouver, the headquarters for the Hudson's Bay Company's northwestern operations.

After four years of declining profits, Smith, Jackson, and Sublette decided to leave the mountains for more lucrative livelihoods. At the 1830 rendezvous, they made arrangements for five associates—Thomas Fitzpatrick,

Jim Bridger, Milton Sublette, Henry Fraeb, and Jean Baptiste Gervais—to buy them out. The new consortium called their enterprise the Rocky Mountain Fur Company (RMF). Unfortunately, although the five partners were master trappers and veteran mountain men, none had the business background to orchestrate a long-term, successful commercial endeavor as complex as the fur business.

Nevertheless, for the next four years RMF—still supported in the field by the rendezvous system that General Ashley had improvised when he first headed into the mountains—became the most famous name in the business, and during its brief lifetime carried scores of well-known trappers on its payroll. However, competition from others, particularly the American Fur Company and two newcomers to the field—Benjamin Louis Eulalie de Bonneville and Nathaniel Wyeth—was ruthless. The five partners watched helplessly as profits declined and as the target of all this activity—the lowly beaver—became more and more elusive.

Both the Bonneville and Wyeth outfits had come to the mountains in 1832. Bonneville was a French-born, American army officer on leave of absence from the military ostensibly "for the purpose of exploring the country to the Rocky mountains and beyond, with a view to ascertaining the nature and character of the several tribes inhabiting those regions." When his leave of absence began in August, 1831, his official mission notwithstanding, Bonneville immediately immersed himself in the fur trade. For the next two years, he and his companions, one of whom was the renowned Joseph R. Walker, went head to head with the other companies in the field. By the mid-1830s, Bonneville was back on regular duty with the army, and his forays into the mountains in search for furs was over.

Nathaniel Wyeth was a Boston ice merchant who wanted to try his hand at the western fur trade, but who lacked the skills to make his efforts successful. During his tenure in the mountains, Wyeth and his followers worked with the Hudson's Bay Company, attempted to be the primary supplier for the Rocky Mountain Fur Company's annual rendezvous of 1834, and tried to do business with Bonneville's organization, all with little success. The dejected Wyeth, after building Fort Hall at the junction of the Snake and Portneuf Rivers, eventually returned to Boston where he continued his career in the ice business.

The Southwest trade was also alive and well during the period of the early 1830s. Charles Bent and his partner, Ceran St. Vrain, organized the Bent, St. Vrain Company, and along with Bent's brother, William, built Bent's Fort along the mountain branch of the Santa Fe Trail in present-day southeastern Colorado. There, for the next several years Bent's Fort became the primary depository for furs trapped out of the southern Rockies and the far Southwest.

In the meantime, the Rocky Mountain Fur Company had changed hands once more. At the 1834 rendezvous, RMF passed from its owners to a new outfit called Fitzpatrick, Sublette, & Bridger. Before the ink on the contract had dried, the firm was defunct, and Fitzpatrick and Bridger hired on with the American Fur Company.

The end of an era was rapidly approaching. Changing styles in men's fashion had witnessed the introduction of silk hats in Europe, and the new look rapidly cut into the demand for beaver fur. It was probably just as well. By the mid-1830s, practically every stream and creek in the American West had been culled by either free trappers or by company men, and the innocent rodent was just about extinct. Although the annual rendezvous continued to be held until 1840, profits from the fur trade dwindled dramatically with each passing year.

By the time the early 1840s rolled around, another type of pioneer was making inroads into the American West. He was the settler, and he was not interested in beaver, or hunting, or exploring. He simply wanted to find a suitable plot of land upon which to support his family. At the time, far-away Oregon was making the news and the fertile lands along the Columbia and Willamette Rivers seemed to be places where a man could raise his crops and his children. By the mid 1840s, scores of wagons and hundreds of starry-eyed immigrants were on their way to Oregon, walking and riding upon the Oregon Trail, a pathway that had been originally charted by mountain men.

In 1843, it occurred to grizzled old Jim Bridger that his glory times in the mountains had come to an end. No more could a man make a decent living in the fur trade. No more could one go for days on end in search of the elusive beaver and never see another human being. No more was there a pristine wilderness untouched by mankind. But old Jim was shrewd, and he knew what he must do to keep up with the times. By now, the Oregon Trail had become the major highway from the Missouri settlements to the great Northwest. Bridger decided to build a fort, but not a fur post like the ones he had frequented for the past score of years. His fort would provide a rest stop for the Oregon Trail travelers.

In December, 1843, Bridger wrote a letter to his friend, Pierre Chouteau, Jr. in St. Louis, in which he explained:

> I have established a small fort, with a black-smith shop and a supply of iron in the road of the emigrants on Black Fork of Green River, which promises fairly. In coming out here they are generally well supplied with money, but by the time they get here they are in need of all kind of supplies, horses, provisions, smith-work, etc. They bring ready cash from the states, and should I receive the goods ordered, will have considerable business with them. . . .

The western fur trade was essentially over. To be sure, individual trappers still roamed the mountains in search of pockets of beaver populations that may have escaped the onslaught of the past two decades. But, by and large, the scarcity of the animal, the decreased demand for its fur, and the mounting numbers of immigrants intent on crossing the Great Plains and Rocky Mountains into Oregon, all spelled doom to the once-lucrative fur business. The torch had passed, and the only vestige of the once-brilliant flame of this important period of national history was the gleam in the eyes of old fur trappers as they rekindled stories from the past.

PART TWO

THE MEN

NO ONE KNOWS with absolute certainty just how many mountain men traipsed the wilderness of the American West during the early and middle years of the nineteenth century in search of the beaver. But, from the time Lewis and Clark completed their "voyage of discovery" in 1806 until the late 1840s, when a greatly reduced demand for beaver pelts—not to mention the critter's near extinction— pretty well ended the fur trade era, hundreds of individuals explored virtually every stream, valley, and mountain top on the spacious map of America's vast trans- Mississippi region.

LeRoy R. Hafen, the editor of the monumental ten-volume series of books entitled, *Mountain Men and the Fur Trade of the Far West*, included 292 biographies. Although this unsurpassed effort brought to light the names and lives of several men of whom few people other than fur trade historians had ever heard, it also missed a few. The point is, we will never know with precision the number— much less the names—of all the mountain men who participated in the western fur trade any more than we will ever identify the number and names of all the thousands of pirates who frequented the high seas.

The purpose of this "Who Was Who" section is to simply provide very brief, although useful, biographies of some (but by no means all) of the men who made their marks on the western fur trade between 1806 and say, 1850. Also included in the list are a few men who, although not "mountain men" *per se,* nevertheless had a profound impact on the fur trade era. Obviously, the millionaire New York scion, John Jacob Astor, was not a mountain man, but his importance to the fur trade is incontestable. Likewise military men, such as Henry Leavenworth and Bennet Riley, were not active in the business, but their relationships and activities with those who were make them candidates for inclusion.

The brief biographies given here are by no means intended to supplant the more comprehensive studies that can be found elsewhere. Hafen's work cited above is and always will be—for the foreseeable future anyway—the absolute final authority on the lives and times of most of the documented mountain men and their associates. But, unfortunately, Hafen's set of books has long been out of print and is virtually unobtainable at any price. It is, therefore, hoped that the following mini-sketches will fill a need for thumbnail information about the nearly one hundred men included here.

◆ JOHN D. ALBERT

John Albert was born in Hagerstown, Maryland, in 1806. Albert was a mountain man who frequented the

"Pueblo," a gathering spot for mountain men located on the site of today's Pueblo, Colorado. When the Taos Revolt broke out in January, 1847, he was visiting with Simeon Turley at Turley's rancho and distillery located at Arroyo Hondo, New Mexico.

Turley's compound was attacked by dissident Mexicans and Indians from the nearby Taos Pueblo, and only Albert and Thomas Tobin eventually escaped the ordeal alive. Albert traveled through the wilderness all the way to his mountain men friends at the Pueblo to advise them of the attack on Turley's Mill and the murder of Charles Bent, the American governor of New Mexico. He later retired to Walsenberg, Colorado, where he maintained a residence until his death in 1899.

◆ **MANUEL ALVAREZ**

Manuel Alvarez was a man who, according to his biographer, Harold H. Dunham, "merits more recognition than he has yet received for his participation in the development of western America." Alvarez was born in 1794 in Abelgas, Spain. An educated man, he emigrated to the United States in 1823. He soon settled in Missouri, where he began his first American profession, that of a Santa Fe trader.

In the late 1820s, Alvarez immersed himself in the fur trade. Becoming a trapper himself, he joined forces with the firm of P. D. Papin and Company, a small French outfit that competed with the American Fur Company along the upper Missouri River and its tributaries. Alvarez attended at least two rendezvous as a free trapper with the Papin Company, which, in the meantime, had entered into a working arrangement with the American Fur Company.

Alvarez appears to have quit the fur trade in 1833 or 1834, and returned to New Mexico. There, he resumed his life as a Santa Fe trader. Over the next quarter century, he participated in commercial enterprises between New Mexico and the United States and was eventually appointed to the post of U.S. consul in Santa Fe. In this position, he worked diligently to protect the rights and welfare of American traders.

A strong supporter of statehood for New Mexico in the late 1840s, Alvarez became lieutenant governor of what was hoped to become the new state in 1850. The movement was thwarted, however, and official territorial status was bestowed on the region instead. Alvarez became a brigadier-general in the New Mexican militia and later the commissioner of public buildings for the territory. He died at Santa Fe in July, 1856.

◆ **WILLIAM HENRY ASHLEY**

William H. Ashley was born in Chesterfield County, Virginia around 1778. He settled in St. Genevieve, Missouri in 1802, becoming a mine operator. Ashley served as a lieutenant-colonel during the War of 1812, moved to St. Louis in 1819, became lieutenant-governor of the soon-to-be new state of Missouri in 1820, and was appointed to the post of brigadier general of the Missouri militia in 1821.

In the meantime, Ashley had formed a partnership with Major Andrew Henry, and in February, 1822, he advertised for one hundred "enterprising young men" to accompany Henry and "to ascend the river Missouri to its source." The 1822 expedition was less than a total success, but a small stockade was built at the mouth of the Yellowstone, while Ashley returned to St. Louis to resupply for the following year. The journey upriver in 1823 became a disaster when Arikara Indians refused to allow Ashley's party to pass their villages. The United States Army was called in, but the affair was resolved indecisively and Ashley lost a great deal of money and time.

General Ashley failed in his bid for the Missouri governorship in 1824, and once again, he headed for the mountains. He hosted the first rendezvous in July, 1825, at Henry's Fork of the Green River. With this initial gathering of Rocky Mountain trappers for the purpose of disposing of their furs and resupplying for the upcoming trapping season, Ashley began a tradition that was to last for sixteen years.

Summer Rendezvous

Willam Ashley personally directed the rendezvous of 1826, at which time he sold his fledgling fur company to Jedediah Smith, David Jackson, and William Sublette. Back home in St. Louis, Ashley continued to serve as the provider of rendezvous supplies to his old company.

In 1831, upon the death of an incumbent Missouri congressman, Ashley was elected to the United States House of Representatives and was reelected in 1832 and 1834. In 1836, he failed once again to win the elusive governorship of Missouri.

William Ashley was an important man in the history of America's westward expansion. One of his biographers, Harvey L. Carter, has written that "Few individuals can be said to have exercised a greater influence on the course of the fur trade of the Far West. . . . The innovations that he introduced can be said to have revolutionized the business."

William Ashley died of pneumonia in March, 1838, and left an estate valued at fifty thousand dollars.

◆ **JOHN JACOB ASTOR**

John Jacob Astor, who undoubtedly made more money in the American fur trade than any other individual, was born on July 17, 1763, at Waldorf, Germany. Emigrating to the United States in 1784, after a brief sojourn in England, young Astor rapidly became involved in the fur business. He was quick to grasp the intricacies of the trade, and before he was forty years old, he had established himself as the foremost fur baron in America.

In 1808, Astor chartered the American Fur Company, an outfit that was to dominate the American northwestern fur trade for many years. American Fur immediately went head to head with the Canadian competition, the North West Company. In 1811, Astor's men founded Astoria at the mouth of the Columbia River, and the Company maintained its control over the region until the settlement was occupied by the British during the War of 1812. After the War, Astor continued to be an important factor in the American fur trade. In addition to his somewhat diminished power in the Pacific Northwest, he wielded tremendous influence in the Great Lakes region.

Following the demise of the United States government factory system in 1822—a coup largely brought about by Astor, his lieutenant, Ramsey Crooks, and the political influence of Senator Thomas Hart Benton—Astor set his sights on the Upper Missouri River. However, his new Western and Upper Missouri Departments, formerly Bernard Pratte and Company and the Columbia Fur Company, respectively, faced stiff competition from the Rocky Mountain Fur Company and its successors.

When the Rocky Mountain fur trade began its decline, Astor's American Fur Company, still in business, turned its attention again to the Great Lakes and to the Great Plains. By 1834, Astor was out of the fur business altogether, enjoying the fame and fortune that he had acquired during his years as head of the largest fur company in America.

John Jacob Astor lived out his days in New York City and died there on March 29, 1848, the richest man in the United States and the progenitor of a family that, in future years, was to have tremendous influence on the social and economic history of the United States.

◆ HENRY ATKINSON

Henry Atkinson's importance to the western fur trade lies in the fact that he was in command of both the first and second Yellowstone Expeditions. The first journey, in 1819, was an effort to warn British traders and their Indian allies along the upper Missouri River that the United States military establishment intended to occupy that region. Unfortunately, the military part of the expedition aborted and got no farther than the mouth of the Platte River. However, the scientific contingent, under the command of Major Stephen Long, struck out overland and successfully explored the eastern front of the Rocky Mountains and much of the central Great Plains.

In 1825, the second Yellowstone Expedition got under way, ostensibly to place a military establishment somewhere between the mouth of the Yellowstone and the Great Falls of the Missouri River. This mission was more successful, and Atkinson negotiated with several Indian tribes along the upper reaches of the Missouri.

Henry Atkinson was born in Person County, North Carolina, in 1782. Gradually rising through army ranks, he was a colonel by the time of the first Yellowstone Expedition. A breveted brigadier-general when the second Yellowstone Expedition got underway, Atkinson returned to St. Louis after the mission and was responsible for the site selection for Jefferson Barracks near St. Louis.

General Atkinson was the senior commander in the Black Hawk War and was in direct command at the Battle of Bad Axe in August, 1832, at which time his army practically annihilated Black Hawk's Sauk and Fox Indians.

Fort Atkinson, located on the Missouri River and previously called Camp Missouri and Fort Calhoun, was named in
Atkinson's honor. General Atkinson died on June 14, 1842,
at Jefferson Barracks, Missouri.

◆ JAMES (JIM) BAKER

One of the later mountain men, Jim Baker was born
on December 19, 1818, at Belleville, Illinois. He apparently did not get to the West until 1838, when he spent a couple of years trapping in the Rockies for the American Fur
Company. Baker returned home in 1840, but by the following year, he was back in the wilderness, guiding emigrants
to the Green River region.

During the next several years, Baker remained in the
mountains among the Shoshoni and Bannock tribes. In the
meantime, he married an Indian woman named Flying
Dawn. In 1857–58, he served as the guide for Captain
Randolph Marcy's expedition from Fort Bridger to New
Mexico and back. Baker settled in Denver in 1859 and
when called upon, he continued to serve as a guide in the
mountains. He moved to Dixon, Wyoming in 1873, and
there he died on May 15, 1898, one of the last of the mountain men.

◆ WILLIAM BECKNELL

William Becknell, sometimes called the "father" of the
Santa Fe Trail, was born in Amherst County, Virginia in
1787 or 1788. By the time the War of 1812 commenced,

Becknell had already emigrated to Missouri, where he served for two years as a United States Mounted Ranger under the command of Daniel Morgan Boone.

In June 1821, Becknell advertised in the *Missouri Intelligencer* for men to accompany him on a trading mission "to the westward for the purpose of trading Horses & Mules, and catching Wild Animals of every description. . . ." The expedition left Arrow Rock on September 1, 1821.

Becknell's outward journey carried him along what is recognized as the primary route of the Santa Fe Trail. Upon reaching the borders of New Mexico, he learned from Spanish soldiers that Mexico had only recently won its independence from Spain and that American traders were now welcome in the country. The party reached Santa Fe on November 16, 1821.

Arriving back at Franklin, Missouri on January 30, 1822, Becknell immediately began making plans for an even larger trading mission to commence later in the spring. Accordingly, "on the 22nd day of May, 1822, I crossed the Arrow Rock ferry, and on the third day our company, consisting of 21 men, with three wagons," began its outward journey. This trip represents the first time that wagons were used on the Santa Fe Trail. The presence of the wheeled vehicles necessitated Becknell finding an alternative path for the last one-third of his trip in order to avoid the treacherous heights of Raton Pass. It was Becknell, then, on his 1822 journey, who pioneered what is now known as the "Cimarron Cutoff"—a route connecting the neighborhood around today's town of Dodge City, Kansas, with Fort Union, New Mexico—that was flatter, albeit hotter and dryer, than the original mountain route.

Becknell made a handsome profit on the goods carried

on his second trip to Santa Fe. He quickly tired of the Santa Fe trade, however, and went west again in the summer of 1824, but this time as a fur trapper, instead of a merchant. Eastern goods had flooded the Santa Fe markets since the Trail had been opened three years earlier, and Becknell thought that a trapping trip into the Colorado and Wyoming Rockies would pay better returns than another trading mission to New Mexico.

Becknell's trapping party was hit by an extremely harsh winter, and in early 1825, he and his men returned to New Mexico, arriving there in April. Proceeding home to Missouri shortly afterwards, Becknell dropped his second career as rapidly as he had his first.

Later in 1825, Becknell was called upon to assist in the official United States survey of the Santa Fe Trail. Later still, he served in the Missouri House of Representatives and as a captain in the Missouri militia during the Black Hawk War. He led a company of mounted soldiers, the "Red River Blues," during the Texas fight for independence from Mexico. Becknell finally settled near Clarksville, Texas and lived a prosperous life until his death on April 25, 1856.

◆ JAMES P. (JIM) BECKWOURTH

"I was born in Fredericksburg, Virginia, on the 26th of April, 1798." Thus begins James Beckwourth's autobiography, published in New York in 1856. His book, *The Life and Adventures of James P. Beckwourth,* has been alternatively praised and criticized by historians ever since its appearance ten years before Jim died. In 1885, the histori-

James P.
Beckwourth

an, Hubert Howe Bancroft described Beckwourth as "a famous hunter, guide, Indian-fighter, chief of the Crows, and horse-thief." Bancroft also added that "No resume can do justice to his adventures, nor can the slightest faith be put in his statements."

Beckwourth was a mulatto. His father was a plantation overseer and a former major in the Revolutionary War, and his mother was a slave. The family name was originally "Beckwith," but Jim later became known as "Beckwourth," and he used the new name forever afterwards. As a young boy, Jim moved to Missouri, where, in time, he was apprenticed to a blacksmith. Later, he worked in the local lead mines, and in 1824, he enlisted with General William Ashley's third fur trading mission about to depart for the upper Missouri River.

During the next few years, Beckwourth pursued his newfound craft in various parts of the Rocky Mountains. Eventually, he was adopted by the Crow Indians and accepted as one of their chiefs. He supposedly married several times within the tribe and often accompanied his Indian brethren on war parties.

During the Second Seminole War (1835–42), Beckwourth fought with Zachary Taylor for at least part of that time. After a horse raiding trip to California in 1840, Jim operated out of Pueblo and Taos. He participated in the suppression of the Taos Revolt in 1847, and went back to California during the Gold Rush.

In 1860, Beckwourth married again and settled down in Denver, where he ran a store and owned a small ranch. Four years later, he guided Colonel J. M. Chivington's Third Colorado Volunteers on their vicious attack upon Black Kettle's Cheyenne and Arapaho encampment at Sand Creek, a deed he later denounced and called "revolting."

Beckwourth's last job was as a scout and messenger at Fort Laramie. Hired to interpret among the Crows for Colonel Henry B. Carrington, Jim finally returned to his adopted people and died in one of their camps in 1866. According to Crow tradition, he was buried on a scaffold.

◆ CHARLES BENT

Charles Bent, the eldest of the four famous Bent brothers who made their names in the western fur trade—the others were William, George, and Robert—was born in Charleston, Virginia (now West Virginia) on November 11, 1799. When he was six years old, Charles moved to St. Louis with his father, Silas, and his mother, Martha. There, in the town that was the gateway to the West, Charles grew to manhood, amid the sights and sounds of the trapper and trader communities.

As a young adult, Charles joined the Missouri Fur Company and spent considerable time on the upper Missouri River, although his exact position with the company is not known. Later, in 1825, he became a partner in the reorganized Missouri Fur Company. The company's poor success, however, caused Bent to look in other directions for his future, and his sights soon became set on the newly opened Santa Fe trade. When his first organized trip to New Mexico rewarded him handsomely, Bent became convinced that the wave of the future pointed to the Southwest. He soon totally immersed himself in a profitable commerce with the remote New Mexican villages.

In 1830, Charles Bent and Ceran St. Vrain, a well-to-do Missouri trader among the Indians of the southern plains, established the Bent, St. Vrain Company, which soon became the foundation of a trading empire that covered hundreds of square miles of modern-day Wyoming, Utah, Colorado, New Mexico, Arizona, Texas, Oklahoma, Kansas, and Nebraska. The company built

Charles Bent

an adobe fort—first known as Fort William, after Charles's brother, and later as Bent's Fort—on the north bank of the Arkansas River, near today's town of La Junta, Colorado.

Charles Bent became so completely absorbed with the southwestern trade that he established a permanent home in Taos, a small Mexican-Indian town north of Santa Fe. He married an affluent Mexican widow, and, although he retained his American citizenship, he involved himself in the civic affairs of the area and soon became a prominent, well-respected resident of the town. In late 1846, when General Stephen Watts Kearny and the Army of the West arrived in Santa Fe and claimed all of the vast Southwest for the United States, Kearny appointed Charles Bent to the office of civilian governor for the territory of New Mexico.

Bent was well qualified for the position of governor since he was so well known and respected in the region. For a short time after his appointment, it appeared that affairs would remain peaceful. However, after Kearny and most of the army left for California to pursue the Mexican War, the civilian population of northern New Mexico became decidedly unstable. Growing suspicious of the Americans and the new reign that followed the military take-over of the area, both the Indians and the Mexicans cast their allegiances to the previous Mexican government rather than support the new American authorities.

By the fall of 1846, revolt was in the air in New Mexico. Charles Bent had only recently returned to his home in Taos from his governor's duties in Santa Fe when he was confronted during the early morning hours of January 19, 1847, by a band of hostile Mexicans and Indians. Bent was attacked and wounded several times

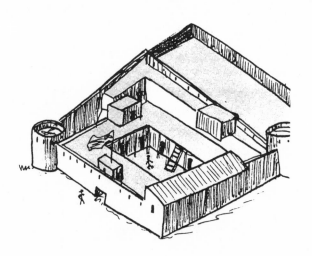

Bent's Fort

and subsequently scalped while he was still alive. Mrs. Bent and her sister, Mrs. Kit Carson, along with the Bent children, escaped the massacre by crawling through a hole in the wall that they had hacked out with a spoon. Caught by the angry mob of attackers in the courtyard, the women and children witnessed Governor Bent's death before their very eyes.

The Bent brothers and Ceran St. Vrain were among the most successful traders on the southwestern frontier. For years their company dominated commerce along the mountain route of the Santa Fe Trail, and Bent's Fort became a Mecca for fur trappers, soldiers, freighters, and southern Plains Indians of several different tribes. Charles Bent, as senior partner of the organization, contributed immeasurably to the westward expansion of the United States.

◆ **GEORGE BENT**

George Bent was born in St. Louis, Missouri, on April 13, 1814, the third of the fur-trader sons born to Silas and Martha Bent. Around 1832, George joined his brothers, William and Charles, in the fur trade business on the southern plains. He assisted in the construction of Bent's Fort on the Arkansas River and eventually became a partner with his brothers and Ceran St. Vrain in the Bent, St. Vrain Company.

Bent worked for several years with his brothers in handling and expanding their business, while dividing his time between the fort and a home in Taos. After the murder of his brother, Charles, in Taos in January, 1847,

George was appointed foreman of the grand jury that heard testimony about the events that took his brother's life. George died suddenly of a fever at Bent's Fort on October 23, 1847, less than a year after the death of Charles.

◆ ROBERT BENT

Robert Bent was the youngest of the four Bent brothers who made such a dramatic impact on the western fur trade. Robert was born in St. Louis, Missouri, on February 23, 1816. At the age of sixteen, he accompanied his brother, George, to Bent's Fort, and there he went to work for his two other brothers, Charles and William.

Whether or not Robert was ever made a partner in the Bent, St. Vrain Company is uncertain, but the younger brother did his tasks around the fort, sharing with George the responsibilities of its management when Charles and William were away. On October 20, 1841, while accompanying a wagon train along the Santa Fe Trail, Robert was killed and scalped by Comanche Indians.

◆ WILLIAM BENT

William Bent, the second of the Bent brothers to leave an indelible mark on the western American fur trade, was born in St. Louis, Missouri, on May 23, 1809, several years after his family had located there from Virginia. William was deeply influenced by his older brother, Charles, who, by 1822, had already established himself as a successful fur trapper and trader among the Indians on the upper

Missouri River. By 1824, William was trapping along the upper reaches of the Arkansas River.

After Charles Bent and Ceran St. Vrain established the Bent, St. Vrain Company in 1830, William was invited to join them as a partner. Bent's Fort, completed in 1833 on the Arkansas River, was originally called Fort William, after the younger Bent, since he was the supervisor of its construction. In time, William became the major driving force in the day-to-day management of the fort's activities, and it was he who guided the company through its successful trading operations among the many Indian tribes of the southern plains.

William Bent married a Cheyenne Indian named Owl Woman. His influence among the Indians, through his marriage, contributed a great deal to the enhancement of peace between the various Plains tribes and the rapidly encroaching whites.

When Bent's Fort was destroyed in August, 1849— either by fire or by William's own hand, depending upon which source one believes—William built a new fort a few miles east of the old one. But, by 1856, weary of a lifetime of trading, he got out of the business altogether.

After the death of Owl Woman, William Bent married twice more, both times to Indian women, and his children observed the traditions of the Indians more than they did those of the whites. When the Colorado militia marched on the Cheyennes in 1864, two of William's sons fought with the Cheyennes, while another was forced to ride with the volunteers. William, himself, was so ingrained with the Indian lifestyle and so loyal to his Cheyenne kinsmen, that he was guarded by troops to keep him from forewarning the Indians of the impending attack.

William Bent, like his older brother, Charles, was a legend among the fur trapping and trading brotherhood of the southern Great Plains. His success as a trader at Bent's Fort has earned him a name, not to be forgotten, in the annals of the western American fur trade.

◆ THOMAS HART BENTON

One of America's foremost promoters of westward expansion during the first half of the nineteenth century was then United States Senator Thomas Hart Benton of Missouri. Benton, who became the first man to serve thirty years in the Senate, was a product of the Tennessee frontier, where he lived as a young man. Born in Orange County, North Carolina, on March 14, 1782, Benton was the son of the former secretary of colonial Carolina Governor William Tryon. Around 1801, Benton, along with his widowed mother, his brothers and sisters, and the family slaves, moved to Williamson County, Tennessee.

The Benton family took up residence west of the small town of Franklin, the county seat, on a several thousand acre estate left by Benton's father and located off the Natchez Trace near the Indian boundary line. Young Benton practiced law in Franklin and was later elected to the Tennessee legislature. In time, he developed a close friendship with Andrew Jackson and was one of the General's regimental commanders of Tennessee forces recruited in 1812 to assist in the war effort.

A falling out with the older and more influential Jackson in 1813 sent young Benton packing to Missouri, where he edited a St. Louis newspaper for a while before getting back into politics, this time as one of the first U.S. senators from the newly admitted state. It was during his senatorial years that Benton wielded such immense influence upon the shaping of the American West. Senator Benton was a leading spokesman for "Manifest Destiny" and was one of a growing number of influential statesmen who believed that it was a natural conclusion for white Americans to conquer and develop the West. And, it was Benton who, with the assistance of Ramsay Crooks and John Jacob Astor's American Fur Company, destroyed the government "factory system" of trade with the Indians, thus leaving the Rocky Mountain region wide open for domination by private trappers and traders.

In time, Benton mended his differences with Andrew Jackson, and throughout much of his Senate tenure, he provided strong support for "Old Hickory." When another Tennessean, James K. Polk, became President, Benton was equally supportive of him and his western land acquisition policies.

Thomas Hart Benton was the father-in-law of John C. Fremont, who in his own time became famous for his explorations of the vast region lying between the Rocky Mountains and California. No doubt, Benton's own keen interest in the West was whetted even more by the illustrious and adventuresome career of the husband of his daughter, Jessie.

In 1850, Benton was finally defeated for his long-held Senate seat, but three years later, he returned to Washington as a U.S. Representative. When he died on April 10, 1858, the American West was on the threshold of a new chapter in its long and varied history. The old days of fur trapping and major exploration had passed, but the time of the cattle barons, the cowboys, the prospectors, the sod-busters, and the settlers was just beginning. No doubt Benton departed this life with the knowledge that it was he who was in large part responsible for the successful domination of the United States over this enormous new country.

◆ BLACK BEAVER

It was not just white Americans and Europeans who were important factors in the history of the western fur trade. Several Indians made noteworthy contributions as well. Black Beaver, a Delaware scout born in 1806 near today's Belleville, Illinois, was one of them.

Black Beaver spent many years in the Rocky Mountains as a trapper, and in 1834, he served as official interpreter for Colonel Richard Dodge when the army met with the Comanche, Kiowa, and Wichita tribes. Frederick Hodge, in his classic *Handbook of American Indians,* wrote that Black Beaver's "services were constantly required by the Government and were invaluable to military and scientific explorers of the plains and the Rocky Mountains. In nearly every one of the early transcontinental expeditions he was the most intelligent and most trusted guide and scout."

During the Mexican War, Black Beaver served as commander of Indian scouts, and after that conflict, he guided immigrant parties across the southern Great Plains. Perhaps his highest honor was the trust placed in him by the Comanches and the Kiowas when these two tribes utilized his services in their negotiations with the whites. Black Beaver died on May 8, 1880.

KARL BODMER

As he tramped through the forests of his native Switzerland, young Karl Bodmer could not have known that, as an adult, he would become one of the foremost artists of the American West. Born on February 6, 1809, at Riesbach, Bodmer studied painting under the tutelage of his uncle, the painter Johann Jakob Meier. When he was nineteen years old, the aspiring artist moved to Koblenz, Germany, where he hoped to be appreciated more than he apparently was in his homeland.

It was while Bodmer was in Koblenz that he came to the attention of the naturalist, Prince Maximilian of Wied-Neuwied. The prince was planning a trip to America, and he was looking for an artist to take along to graphically portray all that he saw on his journey. In May, 1832, the pair, along with the hunter and taxidermist of the expedition, David Dreidoppel, boarded an American ship near Rotterdam and began their voyage to the United States.

The party arrived in Boston in July and, after considerable delay due to a cholera epidemic that was spreading rampant along the eastern seaboard, finally began its westward journey. In the meantime, Prince Maximilian was developing a genuine liking for his Swiss companion. In a letter to his brother, the Prince wrote, "He is a lively, very good man and companion, seems well educated, and is very pleasant and very suitable for me; I am glad I picked him. He makes no demands, and in diligence he is never lacking."

By the spring of 1833, the Prince's entourage was in

49

St. Louis, and from there, on April 10, it headed up the Missouri River aboard the American Fur Company's steamboat, the *Yellowstone*. Bodmer had just missed by a few months meeting another great painter of the West, George Catlin, who had descended the Missouri aboard the same boat the previous year.

Seventy-five days after leaving St. Louis, Maximilian, Bodmer, and Dreidoppel arrived at Fort Union. From there, they took a keelboat to Fort McKenzie. All the time, Bodmer was painting with an intensity that drove him to document scores of landscapes, Indians, and the only known white eye-witness rendering of a battle among Indians, that of the skirmish between peaceful members of the Blackfeet tribe camped outside Fort McKenzie and a party of hostile Crees and Assiniboins.

It is for Bodmer's paintings of several prominent Blackfeet leaders at Fort McKenzie that we owe him one of our greatest debts of gratitude. The Blackfeet had only recently established a fragile peace with the white trapper and trader community, and Bodmer's portraits of many of the tribe's members were among the first ever to be completed.

Downriver, after leaving Fort McKenzie, Bodmer and his party wintered with the Mandans around Fort Clark. He saw and painted many of the same Indians that Catlin had painted a year earlier. It is quite interesting to compare the two men's portraits and their different styles of painting.

After his tour of the American West, Bodmer returned to Europe, never to see the United States again. He produced all of the magnificent illustrations for Prince Maximilian's voluminous treatise on the interior of North America. Although, in later years, he gained some degree of fame as a landscape artist, it is for his careful rendering of the American Indian and the wilderness in which he lived that Bodmer is best remembered.

Karl Bodmer died at Barbizon, France, on October 30, 1893.

◆ BENJAMIN LOUIS EULALIE BONNEVILLE

Benjamin Bonneville was born near Paris, France, on April 14, 1796. In 1803, his mother carried the young Bonneville to the United States. He attended and graduated from the U.S. Military Academy and went on to serve in a variety of army assignments.

On May 1, 1832, Bonneville and a large assemblage of men and supplies left Fort Osage for a trip to the Rocky Mountains. Bonneville had arranged for a three-year leave of absence from the army, and during those three years, he intended to explore the mountains and to trap for beaver.

In the meantime, Bonneville had become acquainted with the famed mountain man, Joseph Walker, and the pair worked together for the next few years. It was Bonneville who sent Walker on the California mission that resulted in Walker's discovery of Yosemite. Bonneville, himself, was responsible for driving the first loaded wagons over South Pass, thus proving once and for all that the formidable Continental Divide was not impassable to vehicular traffic.

Returning to the army after his leave had expired, Bonneville later took part in the Second Seminole and Mexican Wars. He was assigned command of the Military Department of New Mexico in 1855, and during his stay in the Southwest, he saw combat service against the Apache Indians. He also served in a non-combatant role in the Civil War, eventually being promoted to brevet brigadier-general at the conflict's close.

Settling on a farm near Fort Smith, Arkansas, in 1871, Bonneville married a twenty-two year old woman and lived there for the rest of his life. At the time of his death, on June 12, 1878, he was the oldest retired army officer (age eighty-two) in the United States.

◆ ALBERT GALLATIN BOONE

Probably no name is more associated with the American frontier than that of Daniel Boone. But, there were other members of the illustrious Boone family who had an important impact on the development of America as well. One such person was Albert Gallatin Boone, Daniel's grandson.

Born at Greensburg, Kentucky, on April 17, 1806, Boone and his family moved at an early date to Missouri, where Daniel had already migrated. Like old grandfather Daniel, young Albert had a wandering eye. At age eighteen, Boone joined the 1824 Ashley expedition to the Green River, where he got his first taste of beaver trapping. Over the next few years, Boone trapped throughout the Rocky Mountains.

Boone later married and settled at Westport, Missouri. There, he became a trader and supplier for west-bound travelers along the Santa Fe and Oregon Trails. Moving to Denver, then to Pueblo, Colorado, Boone continued his life as a trader, dabbling in politics along the way.

The man whom one historian has declared "should cast a long shadow in any company of westering men," died at La Veta, Colorado, on July 14, 1884.

◆ JAMES (JIM) BRIDGER

Of all the fur trappers and traders who made up the brotherhood of the "mountain men," probably no one lived a more interesting life than Jim Bridger. Bridger was born

James Bridger Monument, Kansas City. *Credit: Idaho State Historical Society, #1010.*

in Richmond, Virginia, on March 17, 1804, just two months before Lewis and Clark left St. Louis on their momentous "voyage of discovery." The two captains could not have known, of course, that in their native state of Virginia, a child was born who would capitalize on their geographical findings to such an extent that he would be recognized in his own lifetime as one of the outstanding authorities on the Rocky Mountains and the West.

Bridger received little formal education, and as a teenager, he was apprenticed to a blacksmith in St. Louis. In 1822, when General William Ashley advertised for men to accompany Major Andrew Henry to the headwaters of the Missouri River, young Bridger eagerly hired on.

On one of his first trips afield, the greenhorn Bridger, along with an older companion, John Fitzgerald, left Hugh Glass for dead after their fellow mountain man had been mauled by a grizzly bear. Bridger, influenced by the older Fitzgerald, finally consented to desert Glass—who seemingly was drawing his last breath—or be left to face the hostile wilderness by himself. Of course, as history has recorded, Glass did not die, but instead survived his ordeal and made his way back to civilization with a vow to kill the two men who left him to the elements. Glass eventually confronted Bridger, but forgave him, chalking up the youth's error in judgment to his inexperience in the wilderness.

In the fall of 1824, while trapping in the vicinity of the present-day junction of the borders of Idaho, Wyoming, and Utah, Bridger, and possibly some companions, explored the Bear River downstream to the point that it emptied into the Great Salt Lake. He thus supposedly became the first white man—or at least one of the first—to visit that heretofore unknown body of water. Upon tasting the lake's salty waters, Bridger is purported to have exclaimed, "Hell, we are on the shores of the Pacific."

After William Ashley sold his fur outfit to Jedediah Smith, David Jackson, and William Sublette, Jim Bridger stayed onboard as an employee of the new company. Later, on August 4, 1830, he himself became one of the principals who bought out Smith and his partners and formed the reorganized Rocky Mountain Fur Company.

Jim Bridger was born in the year that is sometimes recognized as the one that opened the western fur trade. In 1843, after the beaver were all gone and the prairie and plains were choked with immigrants, "Old Gabe" established Fort Bridger in western Wyoming, a post that served as a resting stop for weary westward travelers along the Oregon Trail. The retirement of Bridger from the active fur trade in 1843 signified the end of the "mountain man" era of American history.

Jim Bridger lived to be an old man for the times. He died on his farm in Missouri on July 17, 1881. As one of his biographers has written, how sad it is for today's students of the Rocky Mountain fur trade that no one took the time to interview this true hero of the American West in his autumn years and to record all of the marvelous stories that he could have told. Instead, he lived his later life in solitude, never being visited and, no doubt, casting longing eyes ever westward toward the beloved Rocky Mountains of his youth.

◆ GEORGE W. BUSH

George Washington Bush was a mulatto who was born in Louisiana in 1791. He became an early free trapper in the Columbia River valley, where he was an employee of the Hudson's Bay Company. After his trapping days, Bush farmed in Missouri, and in 1843, he led a party of thirty-two whites to Oregon, where he was refused permission to settle because of his color. He then crossed his party over the Columbia River to present-day Washington, and the little group became the first Americans to settle there.

At the time the British-owned Hudson's Bay Company held jurisdiction over what is now Washington State, and the company's directors frowned upon the American settlement. Since Bush had been a loyal employee of HBC, however, he and his followers were allowed to stay.

George Bush became a well-to-do farmer in the region, and his wheat won the "best in the world" prize at the United States Centennial Fair in 1876. Bush's son was elected a member of the first Washington state legislature in 1889.

◆ ROBERT CAMPBELL

Robert Campbell was one of the better-known foreign-born adventurers who became mountain men. Of Scots ancestry, but born in Ireland in February, 1804, Campbell emigrated to the United States when he was eighteen years old. Two years later he arrived at St. Louis, where he became ill with consumption. His physician prescribed a tour to the wilds of the Rocky Mountains and plenty of fresh air for the sickly youth.

At St. Louis, Campbell became acquainted with General William Ashley and soon found himself an employee of Ashley's fur company. He left for the mountains in November, 1825, on the first of several journeys into the beaver-rich upper Missouri River basin. At the 1832 rendezvous, he participated in the famous Pierre's Hole battle between the mountain men and several hundred warriors of the Blackfeet tribe. In 1833, Campbell and William Sublette began a ten year relationship as partners in a St. Louis-based company whose objective was to supply and outfit free fur trappers at the annual rendezvous.

After the Mexican War, in which he raised and drilled a regiment of Missouri volunteers, Campbell became a successful St. Louis businessman, owning a great deal of real estate in the city. He died in October, 1879, leaving a wife and several children, one of whom, Hugh, survived until 1931.

◆ CHRISTOPHER (KIT) CARSON

The old adage that big things come in small packages is especially applicable to Kit Carson. He was once described by General William Tecumseh Sherman as "a small stoop-shouldered man, with reddish hair, freckled face, soft blue eyes, and nothing to indicate extraordinary courage or daring." According to one of his biographer's, Kit was "the runt of the family." But, size and stature aside, Carson's name is one that comes to practically everyone's mind whenever the western fur trade is discussed.

Carson was born on Christmas Eve, 1809, in Madison County, Kentucky. When still a small child, his family moved to Missouri, where Kit lived for the first fifteen years of his life. Disinterested in school, Carson apprenticed himself to a saddlemaker, and although he got along well enough with his employer, he did not enjoy the work. Accordingly, he broke his apprenticeship contract and headed for the Rocky Mountains.

By late 1826, Carson, now almost seventeen years old, found himself in Taos, a town located on the northern frontier of New Mexico. For the next several years, he worked as a cook, an interpreter, and a driver for some of the many wagon trains that hauled freight across the newly-opened Santa Fe Trail. Around 1829, Kit turned his attentions to the lucrative business of trapping, and for the next several years, he worked the mountains in search of the beaver, rubbing elbows with such eminent contemporaries as Jim Bridger, Thomas Fitzpatrick, Father Pierre Jean De Smet, and Sir William Drummond Stewart.

The next decade witnessed a great decline in the Rocky Mountain beaver population, as well as changes in men's hat styles that lessened the demand for beaver fur. In 1841, Carson hired on as a hunter with the Bent, St. Vrain Company, and the following year he joined the exploration party of Lieutenant John C. Fremont as a guide. In the meantime, he had married a Mexican woman and settled in Taos, New Mexico. Carson was again with Fremont when the 1847 Taos Revolt occurred in which his brother-in-law, Charles Bent, was killed by dissident Mexicans and Indians from the nearby Taos Pueblo.

Kit Carson
*Credit: Idaho
State Historical
Society, #94-B.*

During the War Between the States, Carson served as a colonel with the New Mexico Volunteers, and for a short time, he commanded Fort Union, the U.S. army's largest post in the Southwest, located near the strategic merger of the mountain branch and the Cimarron Cutoff of the Santa Fe Trail. He was noted for his successful forays against the powerful Mescalero Apache and Navajo tribes, and later was brevetted a brigadier-general of volunteers. Carson died in May, 1868, a legend in his own time.

◆ GEORGE CATLIN

George Catlin was a man born to fulfill a mission. Early in life, he had always been interested in Indians. Indeed, his mother, as a young girl, had been held captive by one of the Pennsylvania tribes, and perhaps the vivid stories she told when he was a small boy instilled in him the life-long curiosity he had for his wilderness neighbors.

Catlin was born in 1796 in Wilkes-Barre, Pennsylvania, when that part of the state was still close to the western frontier. Always restless, young Catlin had difficulty deciding what to do with his future. In 1818, he began the practice of law, but soon decided that his real interest was painting. He moved to Philadelphia in 1823 and opened a portrait studio, pursuing a form of art in which he was extremely proficient. Yet, he was not happy at his work. Of that period of his life, he once exclaimed, "My mind was continually reaching for some branch or enterprise of the arts, on which to devote a whole life-time of enthusiasm."

When Catlin once observed a delegation of American Indians visiting government officials in the East, he immediately realized what he wanted to do with his life. "The history and customs of such a people preserved by pictorial illustration are themes worthy the life-time of one man," he noted, "and nothing short of the loss of my life shall prevent me from visiting their country and becoming their historian."

In 1830, Catlin visited St. Louis and accompanied William Clark to Prairie du Chien and Fort Crawford.

Later, he toured Fort Leavenworth and painted among the Kansa villages located on the Kansas River. A year later, he was a guest among the Pawnee, Omaha, Oto, and Missouri tribes. But, it was in 1832, when he traveled far up the Missouri River aboard the American Fur Company's new steamboat, the *Yellowstone,* that he saw his first really "pristine" Indians.

Now, Catlin was in his own element. He painted Crows, Blackfeet, Sioux, and Mandans, all tribes that had experienced little exposure to the westward wanderings of Americans. In eighty-six days on this journey, Catlin painted 135 pictures ranging from portraits of chiefs to landscapes and natural scenes. During the trip, he luckily documented the Mandan tribe, which a short time afterwards was decimated by a smallpox epidemic. In 1834, Catlin visited the Kiowa and the Comanche tribes, and the following year, he traveled to the headwaters of the Mississippi River, homeland to the Ojibway, Sauk, Fox, and Eastern Sioux peoples.

After several seasons of painting west of the Mississippi, Catlin returned East and exhibited his work to the public. His art was modestly received in the United States and abroad, and in time, he had to dispose of most of his paintings which, fortunately for future generations, were purchased by the Smithsonian Institution.

Catlin's value to fur trade history lies in the fact that he captured on canvas the looks and lifestyles of many tribes during the heyday of the trade period, just prior to the introduction of the white man's ways and customs.

◆ TOUSSAINT CHARBONNEAU

This Frenchman's claim to fame probably stems more from his marriage to Sacagawea and his work as interpreter for the Lewis and Clark Expedition than it does for his work as a mountain man. Born in Canada in the late 1750s, Charbonneau was already middle-aged when he agreed to accompany Lewis and Clark from Fort Mandan to the Pacific Ocean and back again in 1805–06.

Several years after his employment with Lewis and Clark, Charbonneau went to work for Manuel Lisa's Missouri Fur Company. Later, in 1816–17, he accompanied Jules DeMun on his abortive trading trip to Santa Fe, where all of the party were imprisoned for several weeks by Spanish authorities. Subsequently he served for nearly twenty years with the United States Indian Department as an interpreter in the upper Missouri River region.

By late 1838, Charbonneau, now eighty years old, was still going strong and married to a fourteen-year-old Assiniboin girl. The following year, he visited his old employer, William Clark, at St. Louis. Shortly afterwards, he dropped from history, and neither the date nor place of his death is known.

◆ AUGUSTE PIERRE CHOUTEAU

A nephew of Auguste Chouteau, one of the founders of St. Louis, young Auguste Pierre was raised amidst the fur-trading community in that gateway city to the West. He attended the U.S. Military Academy at West Point and graduated fourth in his class in 1806. His military career was short-lived, however, and he soon resigned his ensign's commission with the Second Infantry Regiment.

During the first few years of his fur-trading career, Chouteau was active among the Mandans and other tribes along the upper Missouri River. He later became a sub-agent for the Osage tribe and married an Osage woman, before becoming involved with Jules DeMun's various expeditions to the headwaters of the Arkansas River and to New Mexico. Along with several other traders, Chouteau was arrested by Spanish officials in 1817 and held in a Santa Fe prison for forty-eight days.

The combined failure of the New Mexico venture and his less-than-successful entry into the St. Louis business community in the early 1820s drove Chouteau to leave his family and all other interests in St. Louis. He settled with his old friends, the Osages, among whom he lived and conducted business for many years. He was later an active trader with several other Indian tribes, including the displaced Creeks and Cherokees who had recently arrived from the East and the southern plains-dwelling Kiowas and Comanches. Chouteau died on Christmas Day, 1838.

◆ WILLIAM CLARK

William Clark will always be known for his participation and leadership in the Lewis and Clark Expedition. But, during his later life, as Indian agent at St. Louis, he was greatly involved in the western fur trade as well.

Clark, born in 1770 in Virginia, was the youngest brother of General George Rogers Clark of Revolutionary

War fame. He moved to Kentucky as a youngster and, shortly afterwards, joined the army. By 1803, when Meriwether Lewis requested that he share the command of the Expedition, he had resigned from the army and was running the family plantation in Kentucky.

After his second stint in the military and the out-standing success of the Expedition, Clark again resigned from the army and was immediately commissioned brigadier-general in the Louisiana territorial militia as well as U.S. Indian agent with headquarters in St. Louis. Upon Lewis's mysterious death on the Natchez Trace in Tennessee in 1809, Clark was offered his late friend's post of governor of Louisiana Territory, but refused and continued his work as Indian agent. When Louisiana Territory became Missouri Territory in 1813, he became governor, but he was defeated for the post of the state of Missouri's first governor when it joined the Union in 1821. From 1822 until his death sixteen years later, he held the position of superintendent of Indian Affairs and was responsible for the welfare of all the trans-Mississippi River tribes.

In his role as superintendent, Clark was in constant communication with many of the leaders of the western fur trade, and was himself, for many years, a partner in the Missouri Fur Company. When he died in 1838, his funeral procession was the largest public gathering ever recorded in St. Louis.

◆ JAMES CLYMAN

One of James Clyman's most important contributions to fur trade history is the book of recollections that he left to future generations of mountain man aficionados. Clyman was born in Virginia in 1792 on land that his father leased from President George Washington. Later, the family moved to Ohio where Jim saw brief service fighting Indians on the frontier during the War of 1812.

After a brief stay in Indiana and Illinois, during which time he worked as a surveyor, Clyman traveled to St. Louis in 1823 and applied for a job with General William Ashley's second Missouri River expedition. Ashley quickly recognized that the intelligent young man would make a welcome addition to the rough and tumble assemblage he had gathered in St. Louis, and, since Clyman could both read and write, the general hired him on as clerk of one of his keelboats.

Clyman was present during the disastrous attack upon Ashley's expedition by the Arikara Indians and left an important accounting of the affair. After the shaky peace was established with the 'Rees, Jim was assigned to accompany Jed Smith and others to the Continental Divide. On this mission, Smith was mauled by a grizzly bear and it was up to Clyman to patch up the badly wounded Jedediah. In his graphic account of the backwoods surgery, Clyman dryly pointed out that the harrowing experience "gave us a lisson on the charcter of the Grissly Baare which we did not forget."

Clyman's time in the mountains was relatively brief. He returned East to fight in the Black Hawk War, then tried his luck in the lumber business in Wisconsin. He later migrated to Oregon and finally ended up in California where he married and operated a large farm in Napa Valley. Clyman died in California in 1881 at the age of ninety.

JOHN COLTER

Several generations of historians have rightfully called John Colter the "first" mountain man. After all, it was Colter who left the returning Lewis and Clark Expedition in 1806 to set out with two westward-bound adventurers who were heading for the Shinin' Mountains to try their hand at beaver trapping.

Colter was born in Virginia around 1775, but as a youth he followed his family to a new homestead near Maysville, Kentucky. There, in October, 1803, he joined Lewis and Clark as one of the nine "young men from Kentucky," referred to in the official journals of the Expedition. Young Colter was made a hunter for the group, and after a few disciplinary problems in winter camp, he became a valuable addition to the entourage.

After receiving his commanders' permission to leave the Expedition in mid-1806, Colter headed back up the Missouri River with his two newfound friends, Joseph Dickson and Forrest Hancock, bound for the beaver-rich streams of the Rocky Mountains. The partnership soon dissolved, however, and by the following year, Colter had joined Manuel Lisa's trapping party along the upper Missouri River.

Lisa was quick to recognize the value of the young, but experienced, Colter, and he sent him on a mission to spread the word among the neighboring Indian tribes that the newly-built Fort Raymond was open for business. It was while on this trek that Colter became the first white man to see the miraculous hot springs and geysers of today's Yellowstone National Park. For years afterwards, until

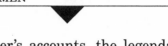

more white eyes proved Colter's accounts, the legendary region around Yellowstone was known as "Colter's Hell."

Although he is well-remembered as an explorer and trapper, Colter's real claim to fame lies in his astounding escape from Blackfeet Indians in the fall of 1808. Colter and a friend, John Potts, were trapping in the vicinity of the Three Forks of the Missouri when they were suddenly confronted by a Blackfeet war party. Potts was killed outright and Colter was taken prisoner. His Blackfeet captors allowed Colter to run for his life, and after he was stripped naked and given a four hundred yard head start, the race was on. In an amazing demonstration of endurance, Colter managed to escape his foes, even killing one of them during the ordeal. Seven days later, the still naked, sun-parched Colter limped through the gates of Lisa's Fort.

In 1810, John Colter left his life in the mountains and returned to civilization in Missouri, declaring that he would "leave the country day after tomorrow—and be damned if I ever come into it again." He kept his promise, settled down, married, and raised a family. Just three years later, the man who had survived the wilds of the Rocky Mountains and the wrath of the Blackfeet Indians died in the settlements after a siege of jaundice. He was only thirty-eight years old.

◆ ROSS COX

Nineteen year old, Irish-born Ross Cox arrived at Astoria, Oregon, in May, 1812, aboard the ship, *Beaver*. He had hired on as a clerk with John Jacob Astor's Pacific Fur Company in New York City the year before. Soon after disembarking at the fort, located near the mouth of the Columbia River, he moved inland with a party of trappers to establish a new fort on the Spokane River. He soon became lost and experienced a harrowing ordeal in the wilderness before he was found by friendly Indians.

Cox left the new post, called Fort Spokane, the following May and returned to Astoria. There he learned that war had been declared between the United States and Great Britain. He also discovered that his company's headquarters on the Columbia River had been occupied by trappers employed by the North West Company, a large Canadian outfit, and that they had renamed it Fort George. With little choice, Cox hired on as a clerk with the new owners.

For the next several years, Cox traveled extensively between Fort George and the interior fur posts belonging to the North West Company. In 1816, he was placed in charge of Fort Okanogan, which had been built in 1811 by Astorians and was the first U.S. settlement in today's state of Washington. In late 1816, although he was still a young man, Cox retired from the fur trade and visited Fort George one last time. He then made an overland journey to Montreal and from there he sailed to Dublin, Ireland, where he married, wrote for a local newspaper, and served as a clerk for the city police department. Neither his date nor place of death is known.

◆ RAMSAY CROOKS

Ramsay Crooks was born in 1787 near Glasgow, the son of a Scots shoemaker and his wife. After his father's death, young Crooks and the rest of the family emigrated to Montreal, before Crooks himself ended up in St. Louis by early 1807. There, in the city that was already deeply involved in the western fur trade—although Lewis and Clark had only returned from the Pacific the previous year—Crooks immersed himself in the Missouri River Indian trade.

In 1810–12, Crooks accompanied Wilson Price Hunt and his overland party from St. Louis to Astoria. One month after he arrived on the shores of the Pacific, Crooks departed for St. Louis as one of Robert Stuart's party of returning Astorians. It was on this trip that Crooks and the others became the first white men to traverse South Pass, although their direction was from west to east.

After his brief sojourn in the mountains, Crooks became a valuable lieutenant of John Jacob Astor, and at one point in his career he owned at least one-fifth and possibly more of the American Fur Company. In 1822, it was Crooks, with the help of Missouri Senator Thomas Hart Benton, who lobbied Congress to abolish the government "factory system" so that private fur interests could get their feet in the door of the lucrative western trade.

Upon John Jacob Astor's exit from the fur business in 1834, Ramsay Crooks bought out the Northern Department of American Fur and continued its operation in the Great Lakes region for several more years. When he died in New York City in 1859, Crooks was known far and wide as one of America's foremost fur men.

◆ JULES DeMUN

Although Jules DeMun was probably one of the most educated, well-bred mountain men who ever frequented the American West, he was one of the most unlikely as well. Born in 1782 in the West Indies of a noble French family, young Jules received a fine education in both England and on the Continent. As a young man, he ran a coffee plantation in Cuba, before emigrating to the United States in 1809. Three years later, DeMun was living in St. Louis and had married into the wealthy and influential Chouteau family.

Determined to support his wife in a manner to which she was accustomed, DeMun entered the southwestern fur trade, having been influenced by the scores of stories circulating around St. Louis about the fabulous fortunes that could be made. DeMun and his men were successful during his second trip to New Mexico in 1816–17, but in May, 1817, they were arrested by Spanish authorities, hauled off to Santa Fe, and imprisoned for seven weeks. To add insult to injury, all of the traders' furs and supplies—worth more than thirty thousand dollars—were confiscated before the party was expelled from New Mexico. DeMun's claim against the Spanish government was finally settled thirty-four years later when all of the principles, including DeMun himself, were dead.

After the New Mexico debacle, DeMun returned to the United States where he managed a general store in St. Louis for a brief period before going back to Cuba and a new coffee plantation in 1819. He reentered the United States eleven years later and operated a trading post in

Wisconsin for a while, served as registrar of the U.S. land office at St. Louis, and discharged his duties as recorder of deeds for the county of St. Louis, the position he was holding when he died in 1843.

◆ ANDREW DRIPS

Andrew Drips, an important player in the western fur trade, was born in Ireland in 1789, but emigrated to Pennsylvania at an early age. He served with the Ohio militia during the War of 1812, later moving to Missouri where he became engaged in the fur business as a partner with Joshua Pilcher in the reorganized Missouri Fur Company. After the demise of Missouri Fur in 1824, Drips stayed in the trade, conducting his business primarily with the Pawnee tribe.

In 1830, Drips joined the Western Department of the American Fur Company and over the next few years trapped across much of the upper Missouri River basin. He attended several rendezvous, including the one at Pierre's Hole in 1832 where the famous skirmish with the Blackfeet occurred. Drips lost a lock of his hair during the battle when a ball ripped through his hat.

Drips was acquainted with and assisted several notables during his career in the mountains, among them Doctor Marcus Whitman, Reverend Samuel Parker, Captain William Drummond Stewart, Captain John Sutter, and Father Pierre DeSmet. Had the timing been a little different, Drips might have gotten the job of guide for John C. Fremont's first expedition, but when Fremont failed to locate him at his home in present-day Kansas City, he hired Kit Carson instead.

After serving a stint as special Indian agent for the upper Missouri River, with emphasis on the control of alcohol among the natives, Drips returned to the mountains as an employee of the Chouteaus. His last involvement with the fur trade was from his post near today's town of Torrington, Wyoming. Drips died in 1860, having participated in the western fur trade longer than most of his contemporaries.

◆ **GEORGE DROUILLARD**

Some historians have attributed George Drouillard with being the first white man to trap beaver in the upper Missouri River basin by virtue of his role as chief hunter for the Lewis and Clark Expedition. Drouillard's exact date and place of birth are unknown, but his father was French-Canadian and his mother was Shawnee. The family lived in Detroit before young Drouillard set out on his own, eventually ending up at Fort Massac, where he was hired for the Expedition.

After his service with Lewis and Clark, Drouillard hired on with Manuel Lisa and accompanied the Spaniard up the Missouri in 1807, where they were met by John Colter, the former Expedition member who had gone back into the wilderness as a guide for two trappers. Colter joined the Lisa party, and after a post was constructed in the fall at the confluence of the Big Horn and Yellowstone Rivers, the two friends were dispatched into the mountains to round up business.

When he returned to St. Louis, Drouillard was tried for the murder of Antoine Bissonette, a Lisa employee who had deserted on the way up the river and whom Lisa had instructed Drouillard to bring back dead or alive. He was acquitted in time to start back up the Missouri in the spring of 1809, again in the employ of Manuel Lisa.

Drouillard's second trip ended in tragedy. For some time, while trapping the region around the Three Forks, Lisa's men had been hampered from intensive trapping due to the presence of hostile Blackfeet Indians in the neighborhood. In May, 1810, Drouillard and a few companions went up the Jefferson River to set their traps and were attacked by a band of Blackfeet. According to Thomas James, who found the body, Drouillard's "head was cut off, his entrails torn out and his body hacked to pieces."

◆ WARREN ANGUS FERRIS

"Westward! Ho! It is the sixteenth of the second month, A.D. 1830, and I have joined a trapping, trading, hunting expedition to the Rocky Mountains." Thus begins the journal of Warren Angus Ferris, a nineteen year old civil engineer from New York. Ferris was not exactly sure himself as to why he decided to risk a bright career on such a risky undertaking. "Why," he wrote, "I scarcely know, for the motives that induced me to this step were of a mixed complexion,—something like the pepper and salt population of this city of St. Louis."

For the next six years Ferris tramped the Rocky Mountains in the employ of the American Fur Company, and while he was busy with his duties, he also found the time to keep a detailed account of his activities. His fascinating journal describes not only the everyday scenes and events in the life of the fur trapper, but also presents a great deal of information about the Yellowstone region and even gives word descriptions of many of the famous mountain men of the day.

After he left the mountains for good, Ferris emigrated to Texas, where he settled the region that would one-day become Dallas. He died at his ranch at Reinhardt, Texas, in February, 1873, almost forty-three years to the day that he started his great adventure into the wilderness of the Rocky Mountains.

◆ THOMAS FITZPATRICK

Thomas "Broken Hand" Fitzpatrick was one of the most prominent of all the mountain men. Born in Ireland in 1799, he emigrated to America when he was nineteen years old. According to the explorer, John C. Fremont, Fitzpatrick received his moniker from the Indians after one of his hands was "shattered" by his exploding rifle. Well educated, but adventurous, the young man joined William Ashley's 1823 expedition up the Missouri River and was present at the battle with the Arikaras.

Fitzpatrick roamed the Rocky Mountains for years, and in so doing rubbed elbows with all of the great and near-great mountain men of the period. At the 1830 rendezvous, he, along with his friends, Jim Bridger, Milton Sublette, Henry Fraeb, and Jean B. Gervais bought out the Smith Jackson & Sublette outfit and called the new entity the Rocky Mountain Fur Company. After that company's failure a few years later, Fitzpatrick joined Jim Bridger, Milton Sublette, Andrew Drips, and Lucien Fontenelle in establishing Fontenelle, Fitzpatrick, and Company.

After retiring from the mountain trade, Fitzpatrick became a guide for immigrants traveling the Oregon and California Trails. His first mission was to escort the 1841 wagon train to the Pacific coast, a job that he performed with impeccable precision. One of the grateful travelers commented afterwards that, had it not been for Fitzpatrick, "probably not one of us would ever have reached California." In addition to helping out weary homesteaders on the westward-reaching trails, Fitzpatrick also guided John C. Fremont on his second exploring expedition to the mountains in 1843.

When war broke out with Mexico in 1846, "Broken Hand" was hired to escort General Stephen Watts Kearny and his Army of the West from Bent's Fort to Santa Fe and beyond. Halfway to California, the army met Kit Carson on the trail and he took over Fitzpatrick's job of guiding the army the rest of the way to the Pacific while Tom carried dispatches from Kearny back to Washington, D.C.

While in the capital city, Fitzpatrick was appointed the job of Indian agent for the Upper Platte and Arkansas Rivers region, a position he filled with dignity, expertise, and understanding. He organized the great treaty-signing at Fort Laramie in 1851, which brought peace to the region until the army violated some of the treaty's articles when they built a series of forts along the Bozeman Trail.

Three years after the treaty, Fitzpatrick again traveled to Washington, D.C. to brief officials on the status of Indian affairs in his region. While there, he became ill with pneumonia and died on February 7, 1854. Perhaps

"Broken Hand's" greatest compliment came a decade after his death when Chief Black Kettle of the Cheyennes exclaimed, "Major Fitzpatrick was a good man. He told us that when he was gone we would have trouble, and it has proved true."

◆ FOUR BEARS (MAH-TO-TOH-PA)

During the 1830s when the fur trade was at its heyday along the Missouri River, Mah-to-toh-pa, whom the traders called Four Bears, was the second chief of the Mandan tribe. The Mandans' two villages, situated near today's Bismarck, South Dakota, numbered about two thousand individuals. When George Catlin, the artist, visited the villages in 1832, Four Bears enjoyed the greatest popularity of any man in the tribe. He was, according to Catlin, "the most extraordinary man, perhaps who lives at this day in the atmosphere of natures noblemen . . . wearing a robe with the history of his battles upon it, which would fill a book of themselves, if properly translated."

Four Bears and Catlin soon became fast friends, and on one occasion, the chief even threw a banquet for the artist. Catlin wrote later that, "Passing his arm through mine, he led me in the most gentlemanly manner through the village and into his own lodge. . . ." and "we enjoyed together for a quarter of an hour the most delightful exchange of good feelings, amid clouds of smoke and pantomimic gesticulations."

Although the Mandan tribe never showed anything but friendship to the white trappers and traders who frequented their villages, their kindnesses were not returned. During the summer of 1837, smallpox was introduced by their white friends, and within several months, the two villages on the banks of the Missouri were all but wiped out by the dreaded disease.

Four Bears was not exempt from the horror. James Kipp, an agent for the American Fur Company, later wrote of his fate.

> This fine fellow sat in his lodge and watched every one of his family die about him (of the smallpox), his wives and children . . . when he walked out, around the village, and wept over the final destruction of his tribe; his braves and warriors . . . all laid low; when he came back to his lodge, where he covered his whole family with a number of robes, and wrapping another around himself, went out upon a hill at a little distance, where he laid for several days, despite all the solicitations of the traders, resolved to starve himself to death.

Nine days later, on July 30, 1837, the great chief of the Mandans died in his lodge, where he had returned and laid down beside his deceased family. He called out his last words in disgust, declaring that he would "die with my face rotten, that even the wolves will shrink with horror at seeing me."

◆ JACOB FOWLER

Although he was a surveyor by profession, Jacob Fowler was well-suited to being a mountain man. Born in Maryland in 1764, he participated in several Indian skirmishes in the old Northwest Territory, including General St. Clair's embarrassing defeat. He later served as a quartermaster with General William Henry Harrison's army during the War of 1812.

By 1821, Fowler had teamed up with Hugh Glenn, a banker friend from his war-time Ohio days, and the two planned a trip far up the Arkansas River to trap and trade with the Indians. The party left Fort Smith in September, and for the next ten months scoured present-day southern Colorado for furs. The Fowler-Glenn expedition is generally credited with founding Pueblo, Colorado, which later became a favorite gathering place for mountain men.

While in the region, the traders learned of Mexico's recent declaration of independence from Spain, and after Glenn traveled to Santa Fe, he sent back word that he had "obtained permition to Hunt to trap and traid In the Spanish provences." The expedition then teamed up in New Mexico and trapped along the Rio Grande and in the Sangre de Christo Mountains, before departing for Missouri on June 1, 1822.

Jacob Fowler died at Covington, Kentucky, in October, 1849, at the age—quite advanced for the times—of eighty-five.

HENRY FRAEB (FRAPP)

Henry Fraeb, sometimes called Henry Frapp, is one of the mystery men of the western fur trade. He appeared on the scene in the late 1820s, but almost nothing is known about his early years or even when and where he was born.

That he was highly regarded by his associates is demonstrated by the fact that he served as a brigade leader for the Smith Jackson & Sublette Company. He later became one of the buyers of his old employers' outfit, which then became known as the Rocky Mountain Fur Company.

Fraeb was present at the 1832 rendezvous and participated in the Battle of Pierre's Hole against the Blackfeet. During the next nine years, he scoured much of the Rocky Mountains, trapped down the Colorado River into present-day Arizona, returned to Missouri for a brief time, and traveled to California with Joe Walker. He was killed in 1841 in Colorado by a joint Cheyenne, Sioux, and Arapaho war party.

HECTOR LEWIS GARRARD

One of the foremost diarists of the American West during the latter days of the fur trade was Hector Lewis Garrard. Born in 1829 in Cincinnati, Ohio, Garrard left his hometown as a youth to visit the Rocky Mountains. In 1846, he joined a caravan bound for Bent's Fort and under the leadership of the eminent Santa Fe trader, Ceran St. Vrain.

After spending several months with the Bent brothers

at their headquarters on the Arkansas River, young Garrard joined a group of trappers and traders in early 1847 for a trip to Taos, New Mexico. There, the band of mountain men avenged the recent murder of Charles Bent by an angry mob of Mexicans and Indians. Before Garrard and his friends left the village, the culprits were brought to trial, and modern-day historians can thank Garrard for his eyewitness account of the court proceedings which sent several New Mexicans and Indians to their deaths by hanging.

During his brief stay in the West, Garrard fraternized with many of the outstanding personalities of the day— Jim Beckwourth, Kit Carson, Lucien Maxwell, St. Vrain, and the Bent brothers. Returning to Cincinnati during the summer of 1847, Garrard studied medicine and opened a practice there. He also found time to write a book about his western adventures, *Wah-to-Yah and the Taos Trail,* which appeared in 1850.

In later years, Garrard became an early settler in southeastern Minnesota, where he practiced medicine. He served in several political and private business roles before again returning to Cincinnati, where he lived for the remainder of his life. Garrard died in 1887.

◆ **ELBRIDGE GERRY**

When Elbridge Gerry was born in Massachusetts on July 18, 1818, the Missouri River fur trade was already nearly a decade old and General William Ashley's famous recruiting advertisement in the Missouri newspapers for "enterprising young men" was only four years in the future. About all that is known of Gerry's early life is the fact that he was the grandson of the earlier Elbridge Gerry who served as vice-president of the United States under President James Madison.

By 1840, Gerry was active in fur trading with the Bent brothers and others, later becoming employed with the American Fur Company. Gerry married a Sioux woman and sired several children with her. By 1860, according to the U.S. census that year, his estate was worth forty thousand dollars and he had six children, aged three through seventeen.

In Colorado, during 1864, after Gerry had warned his white neighbors of an impending Indian attack, his own ranch was attacked and a large number of horses and mules were stolen by the angry Indians. Gerry sued the U.S. government for relief, and his claim was partially settled in 1872. With the proceeds from the suit, he built and operated the Gerry House, a fine hotel located in Evans, Colorado. When he died in April, 1875, Gerry was eulogized as the "first permanent white settler in Weld County."

◆ HUGH GLASS

No one knows for sure when the mountain man, Hugh Glass, was born. By the time he began his illustrious trapping career with the Ashley-Henry party in 1823, he was already being called "Old" Glass by his associates. But, if anyone had reason to look "old," it surely was Glass. Before his entry into the fur trade, he had already lived through more adventures than most men do in a lifetime. He had been a captive of the notorious pirate, Jean Lafitte, and operated as a brigand himself until he outwitted his captors and fled into the Texas wilderness where he took up with the Pawnees for several years.

Glass eventually made his way to St. Louis, where he read William Ashley's advertisement for "one hundred men to ascend the Missouri to the Rocky Mountains." He joined the expedition, along with such soon-to-be notables, Jim Bridger and Jedediah Smith.

As it turned out, Glass's "mountain man" years proved to be even more adventuresome and dangerous than his early days as a captive of Lafitte and the Pawnees. Surviving the costly skirmish with the Arikara tribe in 1823, in which he was wounded in the knee, he volunteered to go with Andrew Henry to the Yellowstone River to trap beaver in virgin territory. It was while he was on this foray that Glass attained immortality among his associates and future generations of fur trade historians.

While he was on a hunting detail for Major Henry, Glass was overcome and severely mauled by a giant grizzly bear. His condition was so poor that he was only given a few hours to live. Accordingly, Henry detailed two men, John Fitzgerald and Jim Bridger, to stay with the old man until he died and to give him a proper burial. But, old Glass wouldn't die. In fact, he clung to life with a tenacity that caused a degree of apprehension for the two men entrusted with his care. After several days of watching over the dying man who wouldn't die, Bridger and Fitzgerald, in fear of being caught by hostile Indians, took all of Glass's possessions and left him to die alone in the wilderness.

Old Hugh's luck came through once again, however.

Through sheer willpower, he survived the ordeal and made his way—first at a crawl, then at a slow walk—over three hundred miles of wilderness until he eventually reached Fort Kiowa. With vengeance on his mind, he finally caught up with Bridger, but decided to spare him due to his youth. Fitzgerald, in the meantime, had joined the U.S. army and claimed protection from the federal government against an angry Glass.

Hugh Glass trapped throughout the Rocky Mountains for several years, and during his own lifetime, his ordeal with the grizzly bear made him a living legend. In his later years, he pursued his trade in the north, around Fort Union, until 1833, when his old foes, the Arikaras, killed him along the Yellowstone River.

◆ **HUGH GLENN**

Hugh Glenn, who, along with his partner, Jacob Fowler, is generally credited with being among the first Americans on the site of today's Pueblo, Colorado, was born in 1788, in Berkeley County, Virginia (present-day West Virginia). In his early twenties, Glenn moved to Cincinnati, where he soon became involved in providing supplies for American troops during the War of 1812. It was during this period of his life that he also met his future partner, Fowler.

In 1821 and 1822, Glenn and Fowler explored the upper reaches of the Arkansas River. When they learned that Mexico had recently declared its independence from Spain, they received permission from Mexican authorities to trap the Rio Grande basin, which they successfully did.

Glenn participated in a couple of later ventures to the West, but his rapidly failing finances sent him back to Cincinnati, where he died in May, 1833.

◆ **MOSES (BLACK) HARRIS**

Not a great deal is known about Moses Harris' early years other than the fact that he was born in South Carolina. According to Alfred Jacob Miller, the artist who painted his portrait at the rendezvous of 1837, he was nicknamed "Black" by his companions due to the presence of "a peculiar blue-black tint, as if gunpowder had been burnt into his face."

Harris was an early Ashley-Henry employee and was present at the great battle with the Arikaras in 1823. He was widely traveled, and in 1826, he supposedly was one of a party of four first Americans to travel around the Great Salt Lake. His tales of the wonders of the Yellowstone region and his sightings of "putrefied" forests in the Black Hills made him a legend in his own time.

On January 1, 1827, Harris, accompanied by William Sublette, left the Great Salt Lake on one of the most grueling trips ever recorded in mountain man history. The pair were destined for St. Louis, where they were to place an order for the upcoming summer rendezvous' supplies. They had only sixty days to make the trip, and after nearly starving to death in blizzard conditions, they arrived four days late. However, General William Ashley, both men's former employer, was the supplier, and he accepted the order from the emaciated trappers anyway.

When the beaver became scarce and changing

fashions made trapping less attractive and lucrative, Harris, like many of his mountain man compatriots, turned to guiding immigrants over the Oregon Trail. He advocated the forceful occupation of Oregon by Americans, and for a brief period, he even resided in the bountiful Willamette valley, where he participated in provisional governmental affairs. In 1849, while he was making preparations in Independence, Missouri, to guide another wagon train across the Great Plains to Oregon, Harris contracted cholera and died.

◆ MARK HEAD (MARKHEAD)

Fellow mountain man, George Semmes Simpson, once declared that Mark Head, who in early literature is often referred to as Markhead, "possessed the most remarkable aptitude for getting into scrapes and out of them in a damaged condition of any man I ever knew." Head, born in Virginia in 1812, came to the Rocky Mountains in 1832, just in time for the big rendezvous at Pierre's Hole where the mountain men got into a fracas with a war party of Blackfeet Indians.

Two years later, when he was with Sir William Drummond Stewart's party, Stewart made the off-the-cuff remark that he would pay five hundred dollars for the scalp of the Indian who had stolen his horse. A short time later, Head came into camp with the bloody scalp and handed it to Sir William.

On January 19, 1847, the day of the Taos Revolt, Head and a companion named Harwood were on their way to Turley's Mill when they were attacked and killed near Red

River, New Mexico by a band of rebellious Mexicans and Indians.

◆ ANDREW HENRY

Andrew Henry is one of the unsung heroes of the western fur trade. While his partner, General William Ashley, is a household name among western historians and aficionados, Henry operated so much in the background that his fame today is far less than his associate's. Henry's exact date of birth is not certain, but is believed to be sometimes between 1773 and 1778. From his birthplace in Pennsylvania, he moved to Louisiana Territory and began operating a lead mine near present-day Potosi, Missouri. When Manuel Lisa organized the St. Louis Missouri Fur Company in 1809, Henry was one of the incorporators.

Henry was with Lisa on the 1809 trip upriver when their party met John Colter and persuaded him to join them and return to the wilderness. The following year, Henry oversaw the construction of a fur post at the Three Forks of the Missouri, and for the next few months, he and his small party combed the upper river basin for furs. Hostile Blackfeet Indians, however, cut short his sojourn at the Three Forks, and while one half of his group returned to St. Louis, he guided the other half further up the Madison River. Later in the year, he established the first American fur post west of the Continental Divide in present-day Idaho.

Fatigued from his hazardous ordeals in the fur trade, Henry retired to Missouri. During the War of 1812, he joined the infantry and attained the rank of major. Forever afterwards, he was called Major Henry. Sometime in the interim between the end of the war and 1822, Henry associated himself with General Ashley, and when the general advertised for "enterprising young men" to accompany his expedition up the Missouri, Major Henry was listed in the ad as the recruiting agent.

Henry and a complement of trader/trappers went upriver in the spring of 1822 and built a small post at the mouth of the Yellowstone River. He was still there the following year when Ashley was confronted by the Arikaras and a fierce battle ensued. By the time Henry and a relief column of trappers arrived at the scene, the conflict was over, and he returned to the fort on the Yellowstone.

Henry stayed in the fur business one more year when he decided in 1824 to call it quits and move back to his farm in Washington County, Missouri. When he died at his home in 1832, a St. Louis newspaper eulogized him as "one of those enterprising traders who first explored the wild and inhospitable regions of the Rocky Mountains," and called him "a man much respected for his honesty, intelligence and enterprise."

◆ WILSON PRICE HUNT

Wilson Price Hunt was the twenty-seven year old merchant whom John Jacob Astor chose to head up his Pacific coast operations. In 1810, Hunt was charged by Astor to travel overland from Fort Michilimackinac to the mouth of the Columbia River where he would construct a fort and become the chief operating officer there. At about the same time, Astor discharged a second group to travel by sea to the same destination.

Hunt and his companions spent the winter at the mouth of the Nodaway River, near today's Missouri, Nebraska, Kansas border. Leaving camp in April, 1811, the group proceeded westward and finally reached the Pacific shores on February 15 of the following year. There, they found that the sea-borne party had already arrived the previous spring and built a fur post appropriately named Astoria.

Hunt later spent time in Alaska and the Hawaiian Islands watching over Astor's fur interests before news of the War of 1812 sent him back to Astoria. When he arrived at the post, he found that most of the other Astor employees had deserted the place, but had left all of the furs and supplies behind. While he was out searching for another ship to rescue the valuables, North West Company employees occupied Astoria and took over its operations. Hunt then returned to New York, via China, arriving there in October, 1816.

Hunt later took up residence in St. Louis where he pursued the life of a merchant until he died in April, 1842.

◆ **DAVID JACKSON**

One of the western fur trade's most brilliant, yet illusive, players was David E. Jackson. Although little is known of the man today, he was a well-respected member of the mountain man brotherhood of the 1820s when the beaver trade was at its peak.

Jackson was one of the hearty group of adventurers who read with interest General William Ashley's 1822 advertisement for "enterprising young men." Although most of the ad's respondents were men in their late teens and early twenties—wild, single, and looking for excitement—Jackson was around thirty-two years old and married, with four children.

Jackson accompanied Andrew Henry up the Missouri River in mid-1822 and helped establish Fort Henry at the mouth of the Yellowstone River. After General Ashley reached the post in the fall with supplies, Jackson left with him and returned to St. Louis. The following year, Jackson was again with Ashley at the hard-fought battle with the Arikaras.

Jackson was present at both the first and second annual rendezvous and became a partner, along with Jedediah Smith and Andrew Sublette, of Ashley's old company when the general sold out to the threesome in 1826. It appears that Jackson administered the day-to-day activities of the outfit, while Smith and Sublette explored and traveled back and forth to St. Louis with the furs.

When he finally gave up trapping, Jackson participated briefly in the Santa Fe trade and was in the same caravan with Jed Smith when Smith was killed by Comanches in 1831. He later did some mule trading in California before retiring to Missouri. In December, 1837, Jackson died of typhoid fever in Paris, Tennessee, where he had journeyed to collect on some investments in the region. Jackson Hole, Wyoming is named for this little- known, yet highly important, mountain man.

◆ THOMAS JAMES

Thomas James was born in 1782 in Maryland but, by age twenty-four, he had moved to Florissant, Missouri, near St. Louis, via Kentucky and Illinois. In 1809, James hired on with Manuel Lisa's St. Louis Missouri Fur Company and, along with close to four hundred other adventurers, started up the Missouri River to trap and to trade with the Indians.

When the expedition had traveled a few miles beyond the Mandan villages, James and a few other Americans quit the company because, as he put it, they had been "taken in, cheated, chiseled, gulled, and swindled in a style that has not, perhaps, been excelled by Yankees or French, or men of any other nation. . . ." After spending a harsh winter on his own as a free trapper, James returned to St. Louis, sold his Florissant property, moved to Pennsylvania, and got married. Returning to St. Louis in late 1813 with his bride, he spent the next two years freighting on the Mississippi and Ohio Rivers.

In 1821, James embarked on a second mountain adventure. This time, he traveled to the head of the Arkansas River, traded with the Indians, and journeyed to Santa Fe where his visit coincided with Mexico's recent declaration of independence from Spain. Becoming disenchanted with the Santa Fe trade, James sold out to his associates and again returned home. He later traded with the Comanches, served in the Illinois General Assembly, became a general in the Illinois militia, and saw limited service in the Black Hawk War. He died at his home near St. Louis in December, 1847.

CHARLES LARPENTEUR

Charles Larpenteur, along with James Clyman and Warren Angus Ferris, was among the few mountain men who left behind detailed accounts of their activities while in the fur trade. A native-born Frenchman, Larpenteur made his way to America in 1818, at age eleven, and for the next decade he resided on a farm near Baltimore, Maryland.

The Frenchman was not cut out to be a farmer, so he migrated to St. Louis in 1828 and hired on with Benjamin O'Fallon, the retired Indian agent for the Missouri River tribes. Five years later, he joined the William Sublette-Robert Campbell outfit with a salary of sixteen dollars a month.

While he was in the field during the first year's outing, Larpenteur changed jobs and went to work for the American Fur Company as a clerk, a job more suited to his education and background than the common labor he had performed for Sublette and Campbell. Larpenteur was filling his clerk's position at Fort Union in 1837, when the great smallpox epidemic hit the tribes along the Missouri River. It is from his pen that scholars today have an accurate account of the malady and its after-effects upon the native population.

Over the next several years, Larpenteur continued his faithful service to American Fur, and in addition to the clerical duties he performed for his outfit, he also led trading expeditions to distant Indian tribes. Inside company rivalries forced him to resign from American Fur in 1846, and for the next few years, he became an independent trad-

91

er among the Flathead Indians. In 1851, he tried retirement on his farm in Iowa and for the next dozen years, he alternated activities between there and the field pursuing the fur trade again. Later, he worked for the government as a commissary escort and sutler, retiring from that job when the army began to enforce a recently passed law that prohibited civilian sutlers on army posts.

After a long and extremely varied life, Charles Larpenteur died on his Iowa farm in November, 1872, and was buried nearby.

◆ HENRY LEAVENWORTH

Although he was a career army man, Henry Leavenworth figures prominently in the western fur trade since he led the military contingent, forever afterwards known as the "Missouri Legion," up the Missouri River in 1823 in an attempt to rescue General William Ashley's trappers from the hostile Arikara Indians. According to some of his contemporaries, his failure to totally subdue the 'Rees when he had the opportunity and his decision to allow them to go largely unpunished for their unwarranted attack only served to strengthen future native resistance to the rapidly expanding Missouri River fur trade.

Leavenworth was born in 1783 in Connecticut. His father served in the Revolution as a colonel. Leavenworth himself saw infantry action around the Great Lakes during the War of 1812. He was a brevet-colonel of the Sixth U.S. Infantry and the commander of Fort Atkinson when he attacked the Arikaras in what was to become the nation's first conflict between the army and a trans-Mississippi tribe.

After the Arikara campaign, Leavenworth went on to other army assignments, among them the establishment of Fort Leavenworth in 1827. He died in 1834 while on assignment near the Washita River.

◆ ZENAS LEONARD

Zenas Leonard spent the first twenty-one years of his life in Pennsylvania. Born on a farm in Clearfield County in 1809, the young man eventually moved to St. Louis, where he took a position as clerk with a fur company. Later becoming a trapper, Leonard participated in the 1832 rendezvous and fought the Blackfeet in the Battle at Pierre's Hole, later writing at length about the event in his useful narrative of the fur trade.

In 1833, Leonard hired on with the Benjamin Bonneville outfit and accompanied Joseph Walker to California, thus becoming one of the first white men to see the wonders of Yosemite. After visiting his home in Pennsylvania in 1835, Leonard returned West and established a trading post near the site of the old Fort Osage factory. He died there in 1857 and is buried nearby.

◆ MANUEL LISA

Lewis and Clark had been back from the Pacific Coast only a year, Jim Bridger was still a three-year old tot playing in Richmond, Virginia, and William Ashley's dreams of a Rocky Mountain fur empire were fifteen years in the future when Manuel Lisa first cordelled up the Missouri River in 1807 in search of the plentiful beaver. Lisa, born of Spanish parentage in 1772 in New Orleans, had already dabbled in the Indian trade in the old Northwest Territory, among the Osage tribe, and in the distant markets of Santa Fe, so he was well prepared to launch this first American assault among the Missouri River tribes.

Lisa's effort resulted in the construction of Fort Raymond at the confluence of the Bighorn and Yellowstone Rivers. The expedition was successful enough that the Spaniard began planning a second upriver journey as soon as he arrived back in St. Louis in the fall of 1807. Two years later, Lisa masterminded the organization of the St. Louis Missouri Fur Company, usually simply called the Missouri Fur Company. His partners included some of the elite of St. Louis, including William Clark, Andrew Henry, Pierre Chouteau, and Reuben Lewis, among others.

For the next several years, Lisa and his struggling company met with mixed success. Cash flow was always a problem, and frequent forays with hostile Indian tribes in the upper Missouri River basin added to Lisa's difficulties. In 1814, the Missouri Fur Company went out of business, and Lisa busied himself with the formation of other partnerships and two marriages, until 1819, when he formed a new Missouri Fur Company.

After the organization of the new company, Lisa had only one upriver trip left. He was stricken with an unknown illness while on that journey and died in August, 1820. The company helm was passed to Lisa's lieutenant, Joshua Pilcher, who ran the outfit for a few more years before it, too, passed into history.

Fort Manuel

Despite the trials and tribulations of Lisa, or the mixed successes of his various enterprises, he was one of the most important men to work in the western fur trade. In some cases, more than any other individual, he laid the groundwork for future generations of trapper/traders and, as such, deserves far more credit than he is usually given.

◆ JOHN C. LUTTIG

History has failed to record exactly when John C. Luttig was born or from which town in Germany he hailed. The sparse facts of his early manhood only reveal that he worked as a merchant in Baltimore before he migrated to Missouri sometime prior to 1812.

It was in St. Louis that young Luttig met Manuel Lisa, the principle organizer of the Missouri Fur Company and, at the time, probably the leading fur trader on the Missouri River. Luttig hired on with Lisa as a clerk and left St. Louis in May, 1812, for a trading mission upriver. When he returned the following year, he unsuccessfully tried to be named the guardian of the son and daughter of Sacagawea, the Shoshoni woman who had accompanied Lewis and Clark from Fort Mandan to the Pacific Ocean.

Luttig's life as a fur trader was short-lived. After his 1813 return downriver, he worked in the St. Louis area, later buying property upon which was discovered a lead mine. He died in July, 1815, before being able to develop the mine. His account of the 1812 journey up the Missouri River with Lisa provides a keen insight into the day-to-day activities of an early trading and trapping expedition.

◆ PRINCE ALEXANDER PHILIP MAXIMILIAN

Although he was not a mountain man, Prince Maximilian's keen observation of Missouri River Indian tribes during the height of the fur trade qualify him for inclusion in this study. Born into an aristocratic German family in 1782, and trained for service in the military, Maximilian eventually rose to the rank of major-general in the Prussian army. His true interest, however, was natural history, and following his army service, he firmly established himself in European scientific circles when he published the results of a two-year-long expedition to Brazil.

In 1832, Maximilian's curiosity turned to North America and he sailed for the United States. Accompanied by the Swiss artist, Karl Bodmer, whom he had hired to graphically capture his upcoming Western expedition, the prince and his party arrived at St. Louis in March, 1833. The following month, the group headed up the Missouri River aboard the American Fur Company boat, the *Yellowstone.*

Prince Maximilian and his entourage got as far upriver as Fort McKenzie, located near the confluence of the Marias and Missouri Rivers. All the time, the prince was busy collecting natural history specimens, interviewing Indians and traders, and keeping copious notes in his journal. Upon his return to St. Louis in May, 1834, after spending the winter at Fort Clark, he departed for New York and then Europe, never to return to the United States.

Maximilian spent the next few years organizing his abundant material, and in 1843, he published an English edition of the resulting study. Today, this first English edition is exceedingly rare. Fortunately, a three-volume, unabridged, annotated reprint of this version was published in 1906, and several abridgments have been produced since. Maximilian's vivid descriptions of many upriver tribes—the Blackfeet, Assiniboin, Crow, Cree, Mandan, Hidatsa, and Sioux, among others—provide valuable insights into the lifestyles and habits of Plains Indians at the very point in time when the natives were becoming corrupted by white men's ways, alcohol, and disease.

◆ **LUCIEN B. MAXWELL**

Lucien Maxwell is perhaps far better known as a New Mexico rancher and land owner than he is a fur trader, but in his early years, he did participate in the southwest

Lucien B. Maxwell

trade, working out of Taos. His Indian clients included the
Utes, Cheyennes, and Arapahos.

Maxwell was born at Kaskaskia, Illinois, in 1818, and
was the grandson of Pierre Menard, a well-known merchant of the region, and at one time, an associate of
Manuel Lisa. As a teenager, Lucien emigrated to New
Mexico, where he became active in the fur and Indian
trade. He worked at one time or another with John C.
Fremont on the latter's first, second, and third exploring
expeditions to the Rockies, beginning in 1842. Fremont
described him as "a resolute man and a good hunter."

In between expeditions, Maxwell married the daughter of Taos resident, Carlos Beaubien, a wealthy judge who,

along with several associates, had been awarded a huge land grant located in northern New Mexico. After the judge's death in 1864, Maxwell inherited the nearly two million acre spread and, for the next five or six years, operated the nearest thing to a baronial empire the Southwest had ever seen, with headquarters at Cimarron. By 1870, he had gradually disposed of most of the land and moved to Fort Sumner, New Mexico where he died in 1875. Interestingly, it was Maxwell's son, Pete, whom Billy the Kid was visiting on the night he was killed by Pat Garrett.

◆ KENNETH McKENZIE

Nineteen year old Kenneth McKenzie arrived in America from his native Scotland in 1816, unaware that within the next two decades he would be hailed as the "King of the Missouri." Going to work for the North West Company, McKenzie moved to St. Louis in 1822, where he helped organize the Columbia Fur Company, becoming its president by 1827, when it merged with John Jacob Astor's American Fur Company.

McKenzie ran American Fur's "Upper Missouri Outfit" for several years, during which time he was responsible for the construction of Fort Union, the largest and best-equipped fur post on the Missouri River. Noted fur trade historian, Hiram M. Chittenden, wrote that "From his headquarters at Fort Union, McKenzie ruled over an extent of country greater than that of many a notable empire in history," adding that he was "universally feared and respected." But when the "King" decided to illegally distill liquor for distribution to the neighboring

**Blockhouse at Fort
Union**

Indian tribes, his fate was sealed. American Fur almost
lost its charter over the infraction, and McKenzie conve-
niently retired from service.

In later years, McKenzie lived off his great wealth,
much of which he acquired in the employ of American Fur,
and ran a wholesale liquor firm in St. Louis, before dying
there in 1861.

◆ ROBERT McKNIGHT

Robert McKnight probably qualifies more as a Santa
Fe trader than he does a mountain man, but the two pro-

fessions overlapped from time to time, so it seems fair to include him here. McKnight was born in Virginia in 1790, and by the time he was nineteen, he had made his way to St. Louis. A decade before the Santa Fe Trail was opened to Missouri traders, he became a partner with James Baird, Benjamin Shreve, and Michael McDonough in order to pursue trade with the New Mexicans.

McKnight's main claim to fame is the fact that when he arrived in Santa Fe, he and his party were arrested and imprisoned. Their goods were confiscated, sold by authorities, and the proceeds were used to pay for their own room and board while in jail! McKnight was held captive for nearly ten years, finally being released when Mexico won its independence from Spain.

After his Santa Fe imprisonment, McKnight continued his trading activities both on the southern Great Plains among the Comanches and in old Mexico. He also involved himself with the Santa Rita copper mines, during which time immortals Kit Carson and James Kirker were employees. McKnight died in Mexico in 1846.

◆ JOHN McLOUGHLIN

There was probably no single individual associated with the western fur trade that was more respected than John McLoughlin. Born in Quebec in 1784, McLoughlin began his long career in the business with the North West Company as a physician. After North West's merger with the Hudson's Bay Company in 1821, McLoughlin stayed on board and quickly advanced in the new organization's management. In 1824, he was awarded the position of chief factor for the company's Columbia district, an area twice the size of Texas, with headquarters at Fort George, formerly the American Fur Company's Astoria.

Shortly after his arrival at Fort George, McLoughlin moved the Hudson's Bay operations several miles up the Columbia River and built a new headquarters which was christened Fort Vancouver. For the next two decades, McLoughin ruled the great Northwest much like a feudal lord in Europe during the Dark Ages. Although he was first and foremost a "company" man whose loyalties to England and the Hudson's Bay Company were paramount, he dealt with American trappers and traders in the vast region with sensitivity and courtesy.

During the early and mid-1840s, as more and more American settlers followed the Oregon Trail to the fertile lands along the Columbia and Willamette Rivers, McLoughlin treated the newcomers with as much kindness as he had their mountain men predecessors. In fact, he often found himself in deep trouble with his employer for assisting the Americans at a time when England was attempting to claim the Oregon country for itself.

When the ownership of Oregon finally passed to the United States in 1846, McLoughlin retired from the fur trade, became an American citizen, and moved to the south side of the Columbia River to Oregon City, where he lived the remainder of his life as a respected and revered friend of his many American neighbors. He died at his home in September, 1857.

◆ JOSEPH MEEK

Joe Meek is probably about as well-known for his work in establishing the United States territory of Oregon as he is for his fur trapping escapades. Nevertheless, the nineteen-year-old Virginian began his long and colorful career as a mountain man in 1829, when he and William Sublette left St. Louis, bound for the Rocky Mountains.

For the next eleven years, Meek worked in the fur trade, and during his time in the mountains, he attended several annual rendezvous, including the one at Pierre's

Joseph L. Meek

Hole in 1832, where the mountain men battled hostile Blackfeet Indians. Later, he traveled to California with Joseph Walker, before settling down in 1840 along the Willamette River in Oregon with his Indian wife.

Meek became a popular and respected farmer in Oregon and soon found himself elected to the post of sheriff. He later became involved in provisional politics. Meek was in Washington, D.C. in 1848—visiting with his kinsmen, President and Mrs. James K. Polk—when Oregon was granted territorial status and he was appointed U.S. marshal. Upon his return to Oregon, he immersed himself into territorial politics, served in the Yakima Indian War, and helped organize the Oregon Republican party.

When Joe Meek died in June, 1875, he was laid to rest on a remote part of his farm. Four hundred people attended the funeral.

◆ **DAVID MERIWETHER**

David Meriwether's long and interesting life covered nearly the entire nineteenth century, and during his varied career, he witnessed the United States grow from a small nation searching for its national identity to an emerging giant among the major powers of the world. Born in Virginia in 1800, Meriwether moved at an early age to Kentucky, near Louisville. In 1819, he accompanied Colonel Henry Atkinson as a sutler on the Yellowstone Expedition to the Mandan villages along the upper Missouri River.

During the following year, Meriwether traveled to New Mexico where he hoped to try his hand at trading with the natives of Santa Fe. For his efforts, he was arrested by Spanish authorities and imprisoned for several months. Upon his promise never to return to New Mexico, he was released and quickly made his way back East. Although he still had an intense desire to travel to the Rockies and to pursue the life of a trapper, his allegiance to his aged parents dictated that he return to Kentucky to care for them.

For the next three decades, Meriwether lived the life of a gentleman farmer, having married in the meantime and sired thirteen children. In 1852, when Kentucky's eminent U.S. senator, Henry Clay, died, Meriwether was appointed to fill the vacancy. The following year, he broke his earlier promise never to return to New Mexico when President Franklin Pierce appointed him governor of that territory. He served in the post until 1857, when he resigned and returned home to Kentucky once more. He died on his farm near Louisville in 1893.

◆ ALFRED JACOB MILLER

Had it not been for a young American artist named Alfred Jacob Miller, modern history would lack a great deal of graphic insight into day-to-day activities during the western fur trade era. Of the many painters who traveled west during the early days of the nineteenth century, Miller was the only one who actually hobnobbed with mountain men at rendezvous. Consequently, his artwork provides a rare look into the trials and tribulations of the fur trapper and his Indian neighbors amidst the pristine wilderness of the Rockies.

Miller was born in 1810 in Baltimore to well-to-do parents. Artistic by nature, the young painter studied portraiture under the famed master, Thomas Sully. Afterwards, he received additional instruction in Paris and Rome. Returning to America, Miller opened a portrait studio in his home town but, by 1837, faced with business failure, he moved to New Orleans. There, he was approached by the British adventurer, Captain William Drummond Stewart, and was hired as staff artist for the captain's upcoming tour of the West.

During the spring of 1837, Stewart, Miller, and their entourage set out for the Rocky Mountains from present-day Kansas City, following the thoroughfare that soon would be called the Oregon Trail. They were guided by the already famous mountain man, Thomas Fitzpatrick. One of the highlights of Miller's journey was his attendance at the thirteenth annual rendezvous, held on the Green River in Wyoming. The wide-eyed artist captured many scenes while there, most of them drawn as sketches that were later used as models for larger, more grandiose paintings. He had ample material at the rendezvous, since it was attended by nearly three thousand warriors from the Shoshoni, Crow, Nez Perce, Bannock, and Flathead tribes, along with several hundred white trappers and traders.

After the trip was over, Miller returned East. He moved to Scotland for a couple of years and lived in Stewart's ancestral castle, where he used his sketches to paint large canvasses for his patron. When he returned to the United States, he settled in Baltimore and lived there until 1874, when he died.

Although Alfred Jacob Miller's stay in the West was brief, his drawings and paintings are the only visual images that remain today of a grand period in American history. The era would have been graphically lost to future generations forever had it not been for his insightful renditions of the life and times of the mountain man.

◆ BENJAMIN O'FALLON

It would have been difficult for young Benjamin O'Fallon to have pursued any other type of career than one associated with the fur trade and Indian affairs. The nephew of General William Clark of Lewis and Clark fame, O'Fallon was born in 1793, in Lexington, Kentucky, and when he was nineteen years old, his Uncle William gave him a job as sutler for the Prairie du Chien expedition of 1813. Three years later, he was promoted to special agent for the Sioux Indians who lived in the upper Mississippi River basin, with his headquarters at Prairie du Chien. Then, in 1818, he transferred to the Missouri River region where he was placed in charge of the tribes that lived along that river.

O'Fallon soon developed a reputation among the Indians and fur traders on the Missouri for being a crusty, hard-to-deal-with agent. He lent his support to the efforts of the American Fur Company and Senator Thomas Hart Benton to abolish the factory system in 1822. He was extremely anti-British, and when Colonel Henry Leavenworth failed to follow up on his Pyrrhic victory over the Arikaras in 1823, O'Fallon even turned his wrath upon Leavenworth and the American army.

Because of chronic ill health, O'Fallon retired from the Indian service in 1826 and lived for the rest of his life at

"Indian Retreat," his farm located near St. Louis. Although he was out of the day-to-day business of fur trading and Indian affairs, he still cherished visits to his home by those who were about to embark on far-reaching expeditions. Prince Maximilian, for one, sought his counsel in 1833 before departing for his trip up the Missouri.

Benjamin O'Fallon died at home in December, 1842, and was buried in the family vault.

◆ PETER SKENE OGDEN

Peter Skene Ogden was born of American parents in Quebec in February, 1790. He began his fur trading career with John Jacob Astor's American Fur Company, working first in the central Canadian region around Hudson Bay, then transferring to the Pacific Northwest. After a disagreement with his superiors at American Fur, he hired on with the Hudson's Bay Company and was placed in command of its Spokane House, located in present-day eastern Washington.

Ogden was active for many years in the Snake River region and the Plateau country. As the ranking Hudson's Bay man in the field, he often came into contact with American trappers, and usually, the associations were cordial. In 1829–30, he blazed a route from Fort Vancouver on the Columbia River to the Gulf of California and back again. For the next fifteen years, he served his company in several positions at posts located further north in Canada, before returning to the Columbia River area around 1845.

Ogden's men helped rescue nearly fifty Americans from the Cayuse Indians after the Whitman Massacre in

1847. He served most of the remainder of his career at Fort Vancouver, working from that post until he quit the business and retired to Oregon City. Ogden died in September, 1854, a symbol of British-American cooperation during the difficult times when control of Oregon territory could have gone either way.

◆ JAMES OHIO PATTIE

With the following words, James Ohio Pattie closed the narrative of his five year sojourn in the American Southwest and California:

> I am impelled . . . to . . . weave a new web of hopes, and form a new series of plans for some pursuit in life. Alas! disappointments, such as I have encountered, are not the motives to impart vigor and firmness for new projects. The freshness, the visions, the hopes of my youthful life are all vanished, and can never return. . . . If there is a lesson from my wanderings, it is . . . one that counsels the young against wandering far away, to see the habitations, and endure the inhospitality of strangers.

Pattie was born in Kentucky around 1804. With his father, Sylvester, and several other adventurers, he left his adopted home in Missouri on a trading mission to the far Southwest in June, 1825. For nearly five years, the group criss-crossed today's states of New Mexico, Arizona, and California, as well as the northern expanses of Mexico.

They trapped their way up one river and down another, garnering beaver from such streams as the Gila, Pecos, Salt, and Colorado Rivers, not to mention the mighty Rio Grande.

Sylvester tried with limited success to develop the Santa Rita copper mines in present-day southwestern New Mexico before he returned to the life of a trapper. His expedition was nearly annihilated by Papago Indians in 1826 and some of its members were imprisoned by the Mexicans in California in 1828, the same year Sylvester died.

During the summer of 1830, James Ohio Pattie made it back to the United States and promptly published the journal of his ordeal in the American West. His later whereabouts and date of death are unknown, but he may have returned to California and lived the rest of his life there.

◆ JOSHUA PILCHER

In 1822, Joshua Pilcher ruled a Missouri River trading empire that employed three hundred men in the field and which grossed twenty-five thousand dollars worth of furs that year. Pilcher was president of the re-organized Missouri Fur Company, having taken over the helm when Manuel Lisa died two years earlier. With previous experience in the mercantile and banking businesses, Pilcher was the natural successor to Lisa.

Pilcher was born in Virginia in 1790, but while he was still young the family moved to the frontier of Kentucky. When he was around twenty-five years old, he moved once again, to St. Louis, where four years later, he signed on as a partner with Lisa and others in the Missouri Fur Company.

In 1823, disaster struck Missouri Fur. While making preparations to return downriver from a long trading and trapping expedition on the upper Missouri River, Pilcher's most experienced trapping party was annihilated by Blackfeet Indians and all furs, equipment, and supplies were lost. The incident spelled the beginning of the end for Missouri Fur, which barely survived the tragedy and could conduct only minor operations for the next few years.

Also, in 1823, Pilcher assisted the U.S. army in General William Ashley's fight with the Arikaras. Volunteers from Missouri Fur were recruited by Pilcher to go up the Missouri River and to assist Ashley, his primary competitor, in the fracas. Pilcher was temporarily made an Indian agent during the melee and, afterwards, was extremely critical of the manner in which Colonel Henry Leavenworth conducted the campaign.

After participating in several other trading efforts in the Rocky Mountains, Pilcher was appointed Superintendent of Indian Affairs at St. Louis in 1838, upon the death of William Clark. He died in June, 1843.

◆ **JOHN POTTS**

John Potts' name lives on in the annals of the western fur trade as the unfortunate companion of John Colter, when Colter was apprehended in the Three Forks region by angry Blackfeet Indians and forced to run for his life. Potts himself was killed in the brief skirmish that preceded Colter's capture.

Potts, born around 1776, was a German by birth and a miller by profession, when he joined the Lewis and Clark Expedition in the fall of 1803. In 1806, after being discharged from the successful expedition's service in St. Louis, Potts went back to the Rockies to hunt and trap on his own. Somewhere along the way he teamed up with Colter, a former expedition member himself.

According to Thomas James, another Manuel Lisa employee as were Colter and Potts at the time, Potts' death occurred when ". . . a party of about eight hundred Blackfoot Indians appeared on the east bank of the [Jefferson] river." Although Colter went ashore as ordered by the Indians, Potts refused to leave the canoe in which he was traveling. One of the Blackfeet shot and wounded Potts, who quickly

> . . . leveled his rifle and shot an Indian dead. In an instant at least a hundred bullets pierced his body, and as many savages rushed into the stream and pulled the canoe, containing his riddled corpse, ashore. They dragged the body up onto the bank and with their hatchets and knives cut and hacked it all to pieces, and limb from limb. . . .

◆ **ETIENNE PROVOST**

Jean N. Nicollet, the eminent French explorer of the land situated between the upper Mississippi and Missouri Rivers and the man who gave John C. Fremont his start, wrote that Etienne Provost was known among his contemporaries as "L'homme des montagnes," or man of the mountains. Indeed, the Canadian-born Provost was renowned all over the West as one of the earliest fur traders in the business.

Born in 1785, Provost's first trading mission occurred when he accompanied the Chouteau-DeMun party to New Mexico in 1815. For his efforts, he, along with the rest of his group, were imprisoned by Spanish officials for forty-eight days. After Mexico achieved its independence in 1821 and welcomed American trappers, Provost made another trip to the Southwest. Later, he trapped the Green River country, and by 1828, he was in the employ of the American Fur Company.

Provost stayed active in the Rocky Mountains during the decades of the 1830s and 1840s. Along the way, he rubbed elbows with many luminaries of American history, including Sir William Drummond Stewart, Alfred Jacob Miller, and John James Audubon, from whom he received fifty dollars a month for his services during 1843.

Provost died in St. Louis in July, 1850. Provo, Utah is named in his honor.

◆ NATHANIEL PRYOR

Nathaniel Pryor was one of the most important men to serve with the Lewis and Clark Expedition to the Pacific Ocean and back again in 1804–06. Born in Virginia around 1772, Pryor was selected for the mission by William Clark and assigned the rank of sergeant.

After his expedition service, Pryor was promoted to ensign, and in 1807, he was placed in command of a small detail charged with escorting the Mandan chief, Sha-ha-ka, back to his people after the Indian had returned with Lewis and Clark and visited Washington, D.C. The mission failed after hostile Arikaras sent the group scurrying back down the Missouri.

Pryor resigned from the army in 1810, rejoined later, and served as a captain with General Andrew Jackson at the Battle of New Orleans, before being discharged in 1815. Until his death in 1830, he traded with the Osage Indians along the Arkansas River and served for a short period as subagent for that tribe.

◆ BENNET RILEY

Bennet Riley is the last of three primarily military men featured in this section, the other two being Henry Atkinson and Henry Leavenworth. The three are included not because they were mountain men, but because they all figured prominently in the fur trade era. For example, Riley, like his superior Leavenworth, was present at William Ashley's fight with the Arikaras in 1823.

Born in Maryland in 1787, Riley fought in the War of 1812 and was a captain of the Sixth U.S. Infantry at the time of the Arikara melee. Service in that conflict was followed six years later by the command of a detail escorting Charles Bent's trader caravan over the Santa Fe Trail, the first-ever escort furnished by the army on the Trail. Bent's wagon train was attacked by Indians and Riley went to the rescue, then waited in American territory for the caravan's return from Santa Fe and escorted them back to Missouri.

Riley later saw service in the Black Hawk and Second

Seminole Wars, before he died in 1853. Fort Riley, Kansas is named in his honor.

◆ ANTOINE ROBIDOUX

Antoine Robidoux, born in Florissant, Missouri in September, 1794, was only one of several members of the Robidoux clan to make his mark on the western fur trade. When he was in his late twenties, Robidoux traveled to Santa Fe and eventually took up residence there. He married a well-to-do Spanish woman, became a Mexican citizen, and settled down to a comfortable and influential life in his adopted home.

Robidoux was responsible for the construction of two fur posts in the Rockies, one on the Gunnison River in western Colorado and the other, called Fort Uintah, located in northeastern Utah. From Fort Uintah, he conducted business with the Ute and Shoshoni tribes, who according to a contemporary "afford some of the largest and best finished sheep and deer skins I ever beheld. . . ."

In the mid-1840s, primarily due to Indian trouble, Robidoux abandoned his mountain forts and returned to Missouri. In 1846, he accompanied Colonel (later General) Stephen Watts Kearny's "Army of the West" from Fort Leavenworth to California during the opening months of the Mexican War. He was wounded in action at the Battle of San Pasqual. He may have lived in California for a while, but later definitely returned to Missouri where he died in August, 1860.

◆ EDWARD ROSE

Of equal importance and influence in the history of the western fur trade as the mulatto mountain man, Jim Beckwourth, was another mulatto, Edward Rose. Rose, born to a white trader father and a mixed blood Cherokee-Negro mother, was raised around Louisville, Kentucky, although his exact birth place and date of birth are unknown. As a youngster, he worked his way to New Orleans as a keelboat hand, and shortly afterwards, moved to St. Louis where he hired on with Manuel Lisa's 1807 expedition up the Missouri River.

During Rose's 1807 trip, he traded among the Crow tribe and quickly became enamoured with the people. Sometime later, he won the everlasting respect of the Crows when he showed outstanding bravery in a skirmish between his friends and a band of Minnetarees. He later worked with Andrew Henry as an interpreter and later still with Lisa's Missouri Fur Company. He saw action at the 1823 Arikara fight with the William Ashley expedition.

For the next decade, Rose lived off and on among his friends, the Crows, but his detailed activities are not known. Mountain man Zenas Leonard reported seeing him in a Crow village in 1834, but that date may be in error since there is some evidence that Rose was killed, possibly by Arikaras, on the Yellowstone during the winter of 1832.

OSBORNE RUSSELL

Born in June, 1814, in Maine, Osborne Russell tried his hand at seafaring, but soon gave up the adventure to pursue a fur trading career in Minnesota and Wisconsin. He joined Nathaniel J. Wyeth's second Rocky Mountain expedition in 1834 and assisted in the construction and management of Fort Hall. He later became associated with the Rocky Mountain Fur Company, then went out on his own as a free trapper.

Russell kept a detailed journal of his wanderings throughout the Rocky Mountains and when he published it under the title of *Journal of a Trapper,* it became— along with the reminiscences of James Clyman, Warren Angus Ferris, and a few other thoughtful mountain men—indispensable in tracing the history of the western fur trade.

After his career as a fur trapper and trader, Russell immersed himself into civic affairs in Oregon and was present at the formation of the provisional government there in 1843. He was appointed judge, but later moved to California during the Gold Rush, where he served as a judge there as well. He operated a shipping business between San Francisco and Portland, but his dishonest partner plunged the company into financial ruin. Russell died in August, 1892, having witnessed the complete settlement of the West.

GEORGE FREDERICK RUXTON

Although he was not a mountain man, nor did he actively participate in the fur trade, George F. Ruxton's vivid narratives of life in the West during the time when the trade was nearing its climax, qualify him for inclusion in this study. Born in England in 1821, Ruxton received early military training, served in the army for a while, and then traveled to Canada. In 1846, he was sent to Mexico as a British attache. Leaving the diplomatic service soon after his arrival there, he then headed north into the American Southwest, where he barely missed the Taos uprising of January, 1847.

The results of Ruxton's extensive travels throughout the West during the late 1840s resulted in two highly readable and informative books, *Adventures in Mexico and the Rocky Mountains* and *Life in the Far West*. He, more than any other writer, captured the *persona* of the mountain man and the unique flavor of his speech. Theodore Roosevelt once wrote that "No one was to equal him [Ruxton] in his portrayal of the Rockies and their Mountain Men. . . ."

After his monumental trip to America and his subsequent return to England, Ruxton made one more journey to the United States. He got only as far as St. Louis, when he was stricken with an attack of dysentery and died in August, 1848, barely twenty-seven years old.

◆ RUFUS B. SAGE

Like George F. Ruxton, Rufus Sage was more of a journalist than he was a mountain man, although he did spend limited time in the Rockies as a trapper/trader. Born in Connecticut in March, 1817, he died in 1893 in the town of his birth. Sage's greatest contribution to the fur trade era was the 1846 publication of his book, *Scenes in the Rocky Mountains,* a volume which the noted Americana bibliophile, Wright Howes, called "an intelligent narrative of extensive travels from the Platte to the Arkansas. . . ."

◆ GEORGE CHAMPLAIN SIBLEY

George Sibley was never a mountain man *per se,* but his influence on the western fur trade epoch as an important and highly successful government factor was profound. Born in 1782 in Massachusetts, Sibley grew up in North Carolina, before migrating to Missouri in 1805 to take the position of assistant factor at Bellefontaine Barracks, near St. Louis. Three years later, he assisted in the construction of Fort Osage, located on the Missouri River near present-day Kansas City.

For nearly twenty years, Sibley held the job of chief factor at Fort Osage which, under his guidance, became one of the most profitable Indian trading houses in the factory system. During his tenure, he negotiated with neighboring Indians and won the allegiance of many tribes in the region. In 1825, he was appointed commissioner of the

Santa Fe Trail survey party and dispensed with his duties admirably.

After retiring from government service, Sibley remained in the area, eventually moving to St. Charles, Missouri, where he died in 1863. After his death, his quite sizable estate there became present-day Lindenwood College. His nephew, General Henry Hopkins Sibley, served in the Confederate Army and was active in Texas and New Mexico during the War Between the States.

◆ **JEDEDIAH STRONG SMITH**

One of the most important mountain men to distinguish himself during the western fur trade period was Jedediah Smith. Jed Smith was born in Jericho, New York, in 1799. In 1822, he responded to General William Ashley's famous advertisement for men to ascend the Missouri River on a trapping expedition. Ashley recruited, in addition to Smith, several other notables of fur trade history. But, unlike many of his contemporaries who often lacked a formal education and who had little use for religious discipline, Smith was a learned man who spoke good English and who possessed strong Christian principles.

Smith was only in his early twenties when he signed on with the Ashley-Henry party, but it did not take long for him to prove to his leaders and co-workers that he was an exceptional young man. He took to the mountains like he had lived among them all of his life, and he quickly became one of the most talented and respected brigade leaders in the entire West. Men twice his age paid him a respect not normally found in the rough and tumble business of fur trapping.

In 1824, Smith led his brigade across the crest of the Rocky Mountains at South Pass. Although this gap in the Continental Divide had first been traversed in the opposite direction in 1811 by the eastward-bound returning Astorians, the real "discovery" of the pass is usually attributed to Jedediah. A few years later he led another group across the desert country of Utah and Nevada to become the first American to spearhead the southern route to California. Other notable feats performed by Smith were the crossing of the Sierra Nevada Mountains and his travels from California to Oregon by land, both deeds being "firsts" for a white man.

Smith eventually left the mountain trade, but by 1831, he faced the sunset again, this time heading to Santa Fe and the desert Southwest, one of the few regions with which he was still unfamiliar. In late May, 1831, Jed's caravan was stranded in the dry desert that lay between the Arkansas and Cimarron Rivers. Smith and Thomas Fitzpatrick rode ahead to find water. Fitzpatrick stayed at the waterhole to await the approaching caravan, while Smith continued his search for more water. He was attacked and mortally wounded by several Comanches, but not before he shot and killed the leader of the Indians. Smith's body was never found.

◆ **THOMAS L. "PEG-LEG" SMITH**

Like the other mountain man named Smith—Jedediah—Thomas was a legend in his own time. Born in

Kentucky in October, 1801, Smith eventually ended up in Missouri. By 1820, he was trapping and trading along the middle reaches of the Missouri River with Antoine Robidoux. Four years later, he struck out in the opposite direction and traveled to Taos, trapped the southwestern streams, and visited among the Hopi and Navajo Indians. He, along with Ewing Young, George Yount, and James Ohio Pattie were among the earliest Americans to trap the rivers of the far Southwest.

In 1827, in northern Colorado, Smith was shot by Indians, and the severity of the wound required that his left foot be removed. Later, when he was fitted with an artificial leg, he earned his nickname, "Peg-leg." Smith's survival for almost forty years after the mishap speaks well for the surgical skills of his companion, Milton Sublette, who amputated the extremity.

Smith's handicap didn't slow him down. Till the end of his life in 1866, he pursued his widely traveled trading career, dabbled in California horse trading, and operated a trading post on the Oregon Trail, where his supplies were eagerly sought by weary immigrants on their way to the Pacific. He died near San Francisco.

◆ CERAN ST. VRAIN

Ceran St. Vrain, who made his mark on the western fur trade as a partner with Charles and William Bent in the far-ranging Bent, St. Vrain Company, was born near St. Louis in May, 1802, the son of French emigrants. St. Vrain's early experience in the fur trade came as a clerk in Bernard Pratt's St. Louis store. Some years later, he headed for the Southwest and eventually earned a name for himself as an honest, intelligent trader in the Santa Fe and Taos areas.

In the early 1830s, St. Vrain and the Bent brothers built Bent's Fort, situated along the Arkansas River on the mountain branch of the Santa Fe Trail. From this distant outpost, located in present-day southeastern Colorado, the partners inaugurated a fur trading empire that transacted business all over the southern Great Plains and that, at one time, rivaled the American Fur Company.

St. Vrain was present during the aftermath of the January, 1847, Taos Revolt in which his friend and partner, Charles Bent, was murdered. When his fur trading days were over and the Mexican War had ended, St. Vrain lived the rest of his years in the tiny New Mexican village of Mora, where he died in 1870.

Ceran St. Vrain

◆ ANDREW W. SUBLETTE

Andrew Sublette was the third of five Sublette brothers to make their marks upon the western fur trade. Born in Kentucky in 1808, Andrew moved with his family to St. Charles, Missouri in 1817. In 1830, he immersed himself in the trade, accompanying his older brother, William, to the rendezvous that year.

Sublette later worked with William as an employee of the Sublette & Campbell Company, then teamed up with Louis Vasquez in 1835. For the next few years Sublette and Vasquez sent trapping parties all over the northern Rockies, and the firm fared well financially. When the fur business showed serious signs of drying up, the partnership was dissolved, leaving Andrew in debt for several years.

After the Mexican War, Sublette settled in California, where he spent the rest of his life dabbling in the lumber and mining businesses. He was killed by a grizzly bear in 1853 near present-day Santa Monica.

◆ MILTON GREEN SUBLETTE

Milton was the second oldest of the Kentucky Sublette boys. Born in 1801, he moved to Missouri in 1817 with the rest of the family. In 1823, he hired on with General William Ashley's second Missouri River expedition and over the next three years made a name for himself among his fellow mountain men. Unlike his brothers, Andrew and William, however, Milton's immediate future lay in the

Fort Laramie

Southwest instead of the upper Missouri River basin and northern Rockies.

By 1826, Milton was trapping along the Gila River and the Rio Grande and among the Apache tribe of Indians. He later rejoined William and worked with the re-organized Rocky Mountain Fur Company for about four years, beginning in 1830. He was present at the Battle of Pierre's Hole during the 1832 rendezvous and later worked with Nathaniel Wyeth's fledgling company.

In early 1835, due to chronic complications from an 1826 wound, Sublette had one of his legs amputated. He adapted fairly well to the cork substitute and attended the summer rendezvous. The following year he, along with Thomas Fitzpatrick, set out to guide the Marcus Whitman party across the Oregon Trail. He had traveled only as far as Fort William (Laramie), before illness forced him to leave the wagon train. On April 5, 1837, he died and was buried in the fort's cemetery.

◆ PINCKNEY W. SUBLETTE

Although Pinckney, next to the youngest of the five Sublette brothers, was called a mountain man, he was only about sixteen years old when he was killed by Blackfeet Indians. Born in Kentucky around 1812, Pinckney had migrated to Missouri with the rest of his family, and in 1827, had joined his older brother, William, on a trapping expedition to the northern Rockies, where his brief life was snuffed out.

◆ SOLOMON P. SUBLETTE

Solomon was the youngest of the Sublette brothers. He was born in 1815 in Kentucky, but grew to adulthood in Missouri. He dabbled in the fur trade for a while, was driven from it by the Financial Panic of 1837, then resumed his trading activities with merchants in Santa Fe.

Solomon accompanied his brother, William, to the Green River country during the 1843 trapping season, before traveling to the Arkansas River region and finally to California. In later life, Solomon served as Indian agent for the Sauk and Fox tribes and participated in a trading venture into old Mexico. He died in Missouri in 1857, never gaining the fame or notoriety of his brothers, William, Andrew, and Milton.

WILLIAM L. SUBLETTE

William was the oldest—he was born in 1799—and most experienced of the Sublette brothers. Like all of his siblings, he was born in Kentucky, later moving to Missouri, where he rapidly established himself in the fur trade. He hired on with General William Ashley's Missouri River expedition of 1823 and was present at the famous battle with the Arikaras.

William was a close friend of Jedediah Smith, and at the 1826 rendezvous, he and David Jackson joined Smith in purchasing General Ashley's fur company, renaming it Smith Jackson & Sublette. In 1830, he transported supplies in wagons from Missouri to the rendezvous site on the Wind River and in so doing demonstrated that the Rockies could be traversed in wheeled vehicles.

Sublette was with his friend, Jedediah Smith, on the Santa Fe Trail in 1831, when Smith was killed by Comanches. This ended Sublette's brief foray into the Santa Fe trade, and he returned to the Rockies, variously working with Nathaniel Wyeth and Robert Campbell in furnishing supplies to rendezvousing mountain men. He was present at the Battle of Pierre's Hole in 1832 and later assisted Sir William Drummond Stewart and Alfred Jacob Miller on their trip to the mountains.

William Sublette died at Pittsburgh in July, 1845, and his body was returned to St. Louis for burial.

◆ THOMAS TATE TOBIN

Tom Tobin, who for years went by his mother's previous name of Autobees, was born around 1823 in St. Louis. When he was still a teenager, he joined his half-brother, Charles Autobees, in Taos, and began living the life of a mountain man. He lived in the Taos area for several years, eventually taking up residence near Simeon Turley's mill and distillery at Arroyo Hondo.

Tobin was with Turley and several other fur trappers in January, 1847, when some five hundred angry Mexicans and Taos Indians attacked Turley's Mill, after murdering Charles Bent and other Americans in nearby Taos. Tobin, along with John Albert and Turley himself, were the only survivors of the attack, and Turley was shortly afterwards killed. Tobin made his way to Santa Fe and apprised officials there of the attack and its grisly outcome.

Over the years Tobin developed quite a reputation as a tracker, and during the 1860s, he ran to ground two wanted criminals, cut off their heads, and returned with the bloody remains to Fort Garland to collect his reward. According to one of his contemporaries, Gwinn Harris Heap, Tobin had "a reputation almost equal to Kit Carson's for bravery, dexterity with his rifle, and skill in mountain life."

Tom Tobin lived longer than most of his mountain men friends, dying in May, 1904.

SIMEON TURLEY

Although Simeon Turley was not a mountain man in the usual sense of the term, his association with mountain men of his era and his manufacture of whiskey used by many traders for their own consumption and for trade with the Indians, qualify him for inclusion in this work.

Born in Kentucky in 1806, Turley, like so many of his state's early pioneers, eventually migrated to Missouri. Then, in 1830, he moved to New Mexico. He ran a store in Taos and built a combination mill and whiskey distillery at Arroyo Hondo, located just a few miles north of town. He quickly involved himself in the lucrative Santa Fe trade and took a common-law Mexican wife. Over the next few years, Turley became an influential member of northern New Mexican society.

In January, 1847, Turley was visited at his mill by a dozen or so old mountain men friends from out of the Rockies. The get-together coincided with a bloody revolt by Mexican citizens of Taos and Indian residents of the nearby Taos pueblo. The American governor, Charles Bent, was murdered, and several other American officials and Mexicans with American loyalties were killed as well.

Shortly after the bloodletting in Taos, the angry mob marched out and laid siege to Turley's Mill. A two-day battle ensued, in which all of the defenders were killed except Turley and two others, who escaped during the second night. A few hours later during his flight from the mill, Turley ran into one of his Mexican neighbors. The man promptly betrayed Turley's whereabouts to the rebels, who proceeded to kill him.

◆ WILLIAM HENRY VANDERBURG

William Vanderburg, a native of Indiana, was born in December, 1800, at Vincennes. Although official records indicate that he attended the U.S. Military Academy at West Point for four and a half years, for some unknown reason, he did not graduate. Soon after he left the Academy in April, 1818, he traveled to St. Louis and there he signed on with the Missouri Fur Company, filling a position at Bellevue, the company's fur post on the Missouri River.

When Joshua Pilcher took over the management of Missouri Fur after Manuel Lisa died, he had a post built in present-day North Dakota and named it Fort Vanderburgh after his young employee. Both the fort and Pilcher's company were doomed to be short-lived after several score of Blackfeet warriors defeated the Immel and Jones party on the Yellowstone River in 1823 and brought financial ruin to the outfit.

During his career in the mountains, Vanderburgh also worked for the American Fur Company, and as a field leader, he went head to head with the Rocky Mountain Fur Company. He participated in the Battle of Pierre's Hole at the 1832 rendezvous. Later, in October of the same year while trapping in the Three Forks region, his brigade was attacked by Blackfeet Indians and Vanderburgh was killed. His body was never found.

JOSEPH REDDEFORD WALKER

Joe Walker was born in Roane County, Tennessee, in December, 1798, less than three years after the region had gained statehood. After spending his minority in the Volunteer State (a name it earned during the War of 1812, in which Walker served under his fellow Tennessean, Andrew Jackson), Joe and the rest of the family moved to Missouri in 1819.

Soon after arriving in Missouri, Walker headed to New Mexico, got arrested, and then worked with the United States commissioners to survey and chart the Santa Fe Trail. He was elected the first sheriff of Jackson County, Missouri, and served two terms before joining Lieutenant Benjamin Bonneville's fur trapping expedition to the Rockies.

While in Bonneville's employ, Walker traveled to California and became the first white man to view Yosemite valley. He attended several rendezvous, and at the 1837 gathering, his likeness was captured on canvass by Alfred Jacob Miller. After the fur trade started its decline, Walker guided westward-bound immigrants, traded in California horses and mules, and accompanied the explorer John C. Fremont on his second expedition. He eventually ended up permanently in California, where he lived the life of an affluent rancher until his death in November, 1872.

◆ EZEKIEL WILLIAMS

Ezekiel Williams is a rather illusive figure in the western fur trade. Born in Kentucky around 1775, by 1807, he had migrated to Missouri and begun the life of an early fur trader with Manuel Lisa. For the next several years he frequented the upper Missouri River in the north as well as New Mexico and the upper Arkansas River in the south, trading there with the Arapaho Indians.

After serving briefly as a ranger along the Missouri River during the War of 1812, Ezekiel returned to his earlier pursuits and worked both with Lisa and as a free trapper. In around 1817, he decided to settle down on a farm near Franklin, Missouri, where a contemporary traveler in the region called him "one of the most advanced settlers of the far west." In 1821, his farm served as a rendezvous for men answering William Becknell's advertisement for his first Santa Fe trading expedition.

Afterwards, Williams moved about Missouri, and at one time or another, he served his community as a saloonkeeper, judge, and postmaster before he died in December, 1844.

◆ WILLIAM SHERLEY (OLD BILL) WILLIAMS

Bill Williams, born in North Carolina in 1787, was one of the more learned mountain men. In 1795, his family moved to a land grant near St. Louis. Although he was educated locally, he, nevertheless, had a talent for languages, and one of his later jobs in Missouri was to serve as interpreter at George Sibley's Fort Osage factory. He

married an Osage woman and lived with the tribe for nearly twenty-five years.

Williams was active all over the West, from the lower
Missouri River to the Blackfeet country near the big
stream's source, and from the upper Arkansas River and
the Rockies' eastern front to Taos, Santa Fe, and even the
Grand Canyon. He rubbed elbows with the Bents, Jed
Smith, William Clark, and Generals Henry Atkinson and
Edmund P. Gaines.

Utilizing his proclivity at languages, Williams com-
piled a two-thousand word Osage-English dictionary for
which he never received credit. Williams was no doubt one
of the more notable mountain men, and when he died in
March, 1849, the brotherhood lost one of its most influential members.

◆ **WILLIAM WOLFSKILL**

Born in Kentucky in 1798, William Wolfskill, like so
many of his neighbors, emigrated to Missouri with his parents. In 1822, he accompanied Charles Becknell on his first
trading mission to Santa Fe and appears to have stayed in
New Mexico for a couple of years trapping, as well as mule
and horse trading.

Wolfskill later worked with the prominent trapper,
Ewing Young, along the Gila River. He then traveled to
California and tried his hand at hunting sea otters, before
permanently settling down near Los Angeles where he
became a prominent figure in the region. He died in 1866
in Los Angeles while operating a successful vineyard and
cattle ranch.

◆ RICHENS LACY ("UNCLE DICK") WOOTTON

Dick Wootton was born in Virginia in May, 1816, and soon after his arrival in Missouri, he hired on with the Bent, St. Vrain Company. For several years he frequented the southern Great Plains between Bent's Fort and Taos. Although he was not present during the tragic Taos Revolt of January, 1847, he later traveled to the New Mexican town and assisted Colonel Sterling Price's troops in putting down the rebellion.

In later life, Wootton built a toll road over Raton Pass

Richens Lacy
Wootton

separating Colorado from New Mexico. He was also instrumental in assisting the development of the Santa Fe Railroad in the region. For his valuable services, railroad management named the first locomotive to cross Raton Pass, the "Uncle Dick." Wootton died in 1893 at his home near Trinidad, Colorado.

◆ NATHANIEL J. WYETH

There were few individuals less suited to life in the wilderness or to the trials and tribulations of the mountain man than Nathaniel Wyeth. Son of a well-to-do Massachusetts family, Wyeth was born near Cambridge in January, 1802. He began his business career at his father's hotel, but he soon found himself harvesting ice from nearby ponds, a business that he helped revolutionize through the development of several helpful inventions.

In the early 1830s, Wyeth became infatuated with Oregon and embarked on an expedition to the northern Rocky Mountains that ended up costing him dearly. He soon found himself in direct competition with men and

Cabin at Fort Hall

organizations much more experienced than he was in dealing with the Indians and finding the best trapping territories. For five years and at a loss of twenty thousand dollars, Wyeth tried to make his naive schemes work, but they were all doomed to failure.

After building Fort Hall on the Snake River and Fort William at the mouth of the Willamette, neither of which captured the fur market as he had hoped, Wyeth eventually returned to Boston and the business that he knew so well. He died in 1856, still with an intense interest in Oregon and the Pacific Northwest.

◆ EWING YOUNG

Ewing Young was born in 1792 on the wild frontier of a region that four years later became the state of Tennessee. As a youth, he received a fair education, hunted and trapped in the foothills of the Appalachian Mountains, and learned the cabinet-maker's trade. Little is known about Young's later years in Tennessee, but by 1822, he had purchased a farm in Missouri and had heard his first stories by returning traders of the fortunes that could be made in far-off Santa Fe.

During his score of years in the West, Young pursued two careers. The first was as a trapper and trader in the American Southwest, followed by the his role as a prominent pioneer and settler of the Pacific Northwest. He was probably one of the best known and respected mountain men in the business, and when he died in Oregon in 1841 at the young age of only forty-nine, the loss was mourned by hundreds of his neighbors.

During the 1820s, Young was active in New Mexico, even applying for Mexican citizenship and operating a store in Taos. This phase of his life also saw him trapping the southwestern streams for beaver and ranging the wilderness as far as California. While on a trip to California in 1833–34, Young crossed the border into the Oregon territory and visited Fort Vancouver, the stronghold of the Hudson's Bay Company, located on the Columbia River. He liked the nearby country, staked out a farm, and opened a lumber mill and a short-lived distillery.

Three years later, Young organized and supervised what was probably the first cattle drive west of the Mississippi River when he and his men drove more than six hundred cows from California to Oregon, thus introducing ranching to the Pacific Northwest. For the remainder of his life, Young was a prominent and influential figure in his adopted home.

◆ GEORGE YOUNT

Like his close associate and fellow mountain man, Ewing Young, George Yount made his most important mark on the fur trade in the American Southwest. Born in North Carolina in 1794, Yount made his way to the Missouri settlements as a youngster. He served in the War of 1812 and later operated a small farm.

In 1826, Yount took his first trip to Santa Fe. While there, he teamed up with Young, and the two of them and their party of trappers scoured the rivers and streams of New Mexico and present-day Colorado for the next two years. In 1829, Yount explored the Great Salt Lake region before returning to New Mexico and Colorado the following year.

In later life, Yount moved to California, where he became an affluent landowner and rancher. He died on his property located in the Napa Valley in October, 1865.

PART THREE

BIBLIOGRAPHY

LISTED IN THIS SECTION is information regarding a large number of books relating to the western fur trade. The vast majority of the titles herein are familiar to the author and have been of extreme value to him in his research over the years. Although the list is fairly comprehensive, some titles, no doubt, have been omitted, either through oversight, or because the author is not personally familiar with them. The publisher welcomes comments and is interested in hearing from the reader regarding suggested additions to the Bibliography for future editions of this book.

Bibliographic data given here usually pertains to first editions. In many cases, however, the first edition has long been out-of-print and unavailable, so, in order to make the list as useful as possible, information is also given regarding reprint editions.

Titles that deal exclusively with the western fur trade and the people who pursued it make up only part of this list. Books wherein the subject is well-covered as part of a larger volume dealing with the broader history of the West are also listed. However, despite the fact that the return of the Lewis and Clark Expedition is generally recognized as the "stepping off" place for American involvement in the western fur trade, Lewis and Clark material in not included here. The list of books about that momentous event is so lengthy that it could comprise a bibliography all its own.

For up-to-date information relative to any book listed herein, it is suggested that you visit your local library or book store and refer to the latest annual edition of Bowker's *Books In Print*. Search techniques in this series, which lists every American book in print at the time, includes "by author," "by title," and "by subject."

Abel, Annie Heloise, Editor. *Journal at Fort Clark, 1834–1839: Descriptive of Life on the Upper Missouri; of a Fur Trader's Experiences Among the Mandans, Gros Ventres, and Their Neighbors; of the Ravages of the Small-Pox Epidemic of 1837*. Pierre, SD: 1932. Reprinted in 1997 by the University of Nebraska Press.

     A reprint of the personal journal depicting the life and times of fur trader Francis T. Chardon and his exploits among the upper-Missouri River Indian tribes in 1837.

_____ , Editor. *Tabeau's Narrative of Loisel's Expedition to the Upper Missouri*. Norman: University of Oklahoma Press, 1939. Reprinted in 1968.

     Documents the 1802–04 Missouri River journeys of French fur trader, Regis Loisel.

American State Papers: Documents, Legislative and Executive, of the Congress of the United States, Indian Affairs, Volumes I and II. Washington, D. C.: Gales and Seaton, 1832 and 1834.

These books—part of an exhaustive series of volumes that deals with early U.S. government involvement in Indian, military, and foreign affairs—preserve several, otherwise hard-to-find, documents relating to the western fur trade between the years 1789 and 1827. Usually, this series can only be found in larger city libraries or state archives.

Ashley, William H. *British Establishments on the Columbia & the State of the Fur Trade.* Fairfield, WA: Ye Galleon Press, 1981.
    A reprint of a rare communication by Ashley and including reports by Ashley himself, Joshua Pilcher, Jedediah Smith, David Jackson, William Sublette, William Clark, and Lewis Cass regarding conditions of the western fur trade during the late 1820s and early 1830s.

Athearn Robert G. *Forts of the Upper Missouri.* Englewood Cliffs, NJ: Prentice-Hall, Inc., 1967.
    This book surveys the setting and importance of all of the upper Missouri River forts and fur posts, as well as a few downriver establishments. Contains an entire chapter dedicated to "The Fur Forts."

Barbour, Barton H., Compiler and Editor. *Tales of the Mountain Men.* Santa Fe: The Press of the Palace of the Governors, 1984.
    A brief collection of stories about the trials and tribulations of mountain men, including Jed Smith's confrontation with the grizzly, Hugh Glass's ordeal in the wilderness, and Moses "Black" Harris' visit to the "Putrefied" Forest. This volume was published in a very limited edition and might be difficult to find.

Bartlett, Richard A. and Goetzmann, William H. *Exploring the American West, 1803–1879.* Washington, D. C: National Park Service, 1982.
    One of the U.S. National Park Service's newly

designed "Handbooks" to its properties, this well-illustrated (in full color) book highlights the mountain men's achievements as leading elements in the exploration of the American West.

Batman, Richard. *American Ecclesiastes: The Stories of James Pattie.* San Diego: Harcourt Brace Jovanovich, Publishers, 1984.
    Using Pattie's personal diary as his primary source, Batman documents the Kentucky-born mountain man's epic journey to present-day California, Mexico, and the American Southwest during the 1820s.

Beachum, Larry M. *William Becknell: Father of the Santa Fe Trade.* El Paso: Texas Western Press, 1982.
    A brief biography of William Becknell. Although he is remembered primarily for the opening of the Santa Fe Trail in 1821, Becknell did try his hand—unsuccessfully—in the fur trade several years later.

Berry, Don. *A Majority of Scoundrels.* New York: Harper & Brothers, 1961. Reprinted in 1990 by Comstock Editions.
    Provides the best all-around look at the history of the Rocky Mountain Fur Company and its predecessors. The first edition contains two over-sized maps that depict fur trapping and trading regions of interest. A "must" volume in any fur-trade library.

Blevins, Winfred. *Give Your Heart to the Hawks.* New York: Nash Publishing Company, 1973. Reprinted in 1995 by Tamarack Books, Inc., Boise, ID.
    An excellent introduction to the western fur trade period and the men who pursued it, using extensive quotations from the writings of the mountain men themselves.

Bonner, T. D. *The Life and Adventures of James P. Beckwourth, Mountaineer, Scout, and Pioneer, and Chief of the Crow Nation of Indians.* New York: Harper & Brothers, Publishers, 1856. Reprinted in 1972 by the University of Nebraska Press.

THE

LIFE AND ADVENTURES

OF

JAMES P. BECKWOURTH,

MOUNTAINEER, SCOUT, AND PIONEER,

AND

CHIEF OF THE CROW NATION OF INDIANS.

With Illustrations.

WRITTEN FROM HIS OWN DICTATION,

BY T. D. BONNER.

NEW YORK:

HARPER & BROTHERS, PUBLISHERS,

FRANKLIN SQUARE.

1856.

A partial biography (he was still living when the book was published) of the celebrated mulatto mountain man, Jim Beckwourth, one of the true legends of the mountain trade. Beckwourth's veracity has often been called to task by modern scholars, and even though the book is obviously embellished here and there, it remains a good reference for important events as recalled by someone who was actually present at the time they occurred.

Brooks, George R., Editor. *The Southwest Expedition of Jedediah S. Smith: His Personal Account of the Journey to California, 1826–1827.* Glendale: The Arthur H. Clark Company, 1977. Reprinted in 1989 by the University of Nebraska Press.

The title of this book says it all. Provides a balanced picture of this important phase of Smith's life, shortly before his untimely murder on the Santa Fe Trail.

Brown, Dee. *The Westerners.* New York: Holt, Rinehart and
Winston, 1974.

Written by the author of the award-winning *Bury My
Heart at Wounded Knee,* this book contains a well-done,
generalized history of the exploration and settlement of the
Old West, including a chapter about the fur trade entitled,
"Knight in Buckskins."

Carson, Christopher (Kit). Edited by Milo M. Quaife. *Kit
Carson's Autobiography.* Lincoln: University of Nebraska
Press, 1966.

The famed mountain man's own story, including
accounts of his trapping expedition to California in 1829–31
with Ewing Young and his duel at the 1837 Green River
rendezvous.

Catlin, George. *Letters and Notes on the Manners, Customs and
Conditions of the North American Indians.* London: The
Author, 1841.

This book has been reprinted many times by many
publishers over the years. Catlin was one of three better-
known artists—the others were Karl Bodmer and Alfred
Jacob Miller—who traveled West during the 1830s and captured Indian life as it was before its long mid-century
decline. Although he did not particularly fraternize with
mountain men, Catlin's verbal and visual accounts of several Plains Indian tribes are invaluable to a study of the
trans-Mississippi fur trade.

Chittenden, Hiram Martin. *The American Fur Trade of the Far West*. New York: Francis P. Harper, 1902. Reprinted several times over the years, the last time in 1986 (in two volumes) by the University of Nebraska Press.

Even after almost a century, Chittenden's three-volume study is still, by far, the most informative book ever written about the western fur trade. For several years, the author researched a wealth of source documentation at a time when it was far easier to obtain than it is today. No fur-trade library can be called complete without these important volumes.

THE

American Fur Trade

OF THE

Far West

A History of the Pioneer Trading Posts and Early Fur Companies of the Missouri Valley and the Rocky Mountains and of the Overland Commerce with Santa Fe.

MAP AND ILLUSTRATIONS

BY

HIRAM MARTIN CHITTENDEN

Captain Corps of Engineers, U. S. A., Author of "The Yellowstone."

THREE VOLUMES

VOLUME I.

NEW YORK
FRANCIS P. HARPER
1902

Cleland, Robert Glass. *This Reckless Breed of Men: The Trappers and Traders of the Southwest*. New York: Alfred A. Knopf, 1950. Reprinted in 1992 by the University of Nebraska Press.

Cleland's book joins David Weber's *The Taos Traders,* (see entry below) as one of the few book-length studies of the southwestern fur trade, a period often overshadowed by the more popular upper Missouri River and northern Rocky Mountain trade.

Cline, Gloria G. *Peter Skene Ogden.* Norman: University of Oklahoma Press, 1974.

A well-done biography of Ogden, an early employee of the Hudson's Bay Company during its operations in the American Northwest.

Clokey, Richard M. *William H. Ashley: Enterprise and Politics in the Trans-Mississippi West.* Norman: University of Oklahoma Press, 1980.

Explores the political and economic aspects of the Rocky Mountain fur trade and the man who revolutionized the industry by his introduction of the "rendezvous" system.

Clyman, James. Edited by Linda M. Hasselstrom. *Journal of a Mountain Man.* Missoula, MT: Mountain Press Publishing Company, 1984.

Clyman was one of only a handful of mountain men who left behind remembrances of the fur trade era. His recollections give extremely valuable insights into the activities of the Ashley-Henry outfit during its early days on the upper Missouri River.

Coblentz, Stanton A. *The Swallowing Wilderness. The Life of a Frontiersman: James Ohio Pattie.* New York, 1961.

A modern-day account, based on Pattie's original narrative, of the Kentucky fur trapper's adventures in the Southwest during the late 1820s.

Conard, Howard L. *"Uncle Dick" Wootton.* Chicago: W. E. Dibble & Co., 1890. Reprinted in 1980 by Time-Life Books.

"Uncle Dick" Wootton

THE PIONEER FRONTIERSMAN OF THE ROCKY
MOUNTAIN REGION

AN ACCOUNT OF THE ADVENTURES AND THRILLING
EXPERIENCES OF THE MOST NOTED AMERICAN
HUNTER, TRAPPER, GUIDE, SCOUT, AND
INDIAN FIGHTER NOW LIVING

BY
HOWARD LOUIS CONARD

WITH AN INTRODUCTION
BY
MAJ. JOSEPH KIRKLAND

CHICAGO
W. E. DIBBLE & CO
1890

An interesting biography of a mountain man whose life spanned many decades of Western development, from the closing days of the fur trade in the late 1840s to the appearance of the Santa Fe railroad in the Southwest many years later.

Coues, Elliot, Editor. *The Journal of Jacob Fowler.* New York: Francis P. Harper, 1898. Reprinted in 1965 by Ross & Haines, Inc.

Documents, in Fowler's own words, his 1821–22 trading and trapping journey with Hugh Glenn and others from Arkansas to the sources of the Arkansas River and the Rio Grande. In the process, Fowler's trappers became the first white men to explcre the site of present-day Pueblo, Colorado.

Coyner, David H. *The Lost Trappers: A Collection of Interesting Scenes and Events in the Rocky Mountains.* Cincinnati: J.A. & U.P. James, 1847. Reprinted in 1970 by the University of New Mexico Press.

American history authorities maintain that this book sometimes stretches the truth. Nevertheless, it does provide important information regarding mountain man Ezekiel Williams' early exploration in the Rocky

Mountains. David Weber's introduction to the 1970 reprint places the book in proper perspective in light of modern-day research and knowledge.

Crutchfield, James A. *A Primer of the North American Fur Trade.* Union City, TN: Pioneer Press, 1986.
   A profusely illustrated, introductory book into various facets of the fur trade, with emphasis on the West. Subjects covered include arms, equipment, shelter, mountain men, boats, and the rendezvous, among others.

_____ ., O'Neal, Bill, and Walker, Dale. *Legends of the Wild West.* Lincolnwood, IL: Publications International, 1995.
   A magnificent, beautifully produced, four-color coffee table book that includes a section on mountain men in general, along with brief biographies of several notables, including Jim Bridger, Kit Carson, and Joe Meek, among others.

Dale, Harrison Clifford. *The Explorations of William H. Ashley and Jedediah Smith, 1822–1829.* Lincoln: University of Nebraska Press, 1991.
   Traces the travels of Ashley and Smith during their period of close association and involvement in the Rocky Mountain trade.

Davis, William C. *The American Frontier: Pioneers, Settlers & Cowboys 1800–1899.* London: Salamander Books, Ltd., 1992.
   A large-format, pictorial work based on the collections of the world-renowned Buffalo Bill Historical Center in Cody, Wyoming. Contains some material on the western fur trade period.

DeVoto, Bernard. *Across the Wide Missouri.* New York: Houghton Mifflin, 1947. Reprinted many times by various publishers.

A classic account of the closing days of the Rocky Mountain fur trade era, with special emphasis on the Scots sportsman, William Drummond Stewart, and his artist-companion, Alfred Jacob Miller, who together witnessed and documented in words and on canvass this monumental period in American history. A "must have" volume in any fur-trade book collection.

Dippie, Brian W. *Catlin and His Contemporaries: The Politics of Patronage.* Lincoln: University of Nebraska Press, 1990.

Although this book has little to do with the fur trade, *per se,* it is, nonetheless, interesting, since it shows how the famous artist, George Catlin—along with fellow painters, Karl Bodmer, Alfred Jacob Miller, and others—vied with each other for public support and government patronage for their collections. All three men were active on the western frontier during fur trade times, and one of them, Alfred Jacob Miller, became the only artist to leave visual eyewitness accounts of fur trade activities.

Donnelly, Joseph P., Editor. *Wilderness Kingdom: The Journals & Paintings of Nicolas Point, S. J.* New York: Holt, Rinehart and Winston, 1967.

This book presents a never-before-published translation of Father Nicolas Point's journals kept while he lived among the Indian tribes of the Rocky Mountains during the 1840s. Illustrated with Point's own paintings, its pages provide first-hand information about the customs of these tribes during the last days of the Rocky Mountain fur trade.

Dryden, Cecil. *Up the Columbia for Furs.* Caldwell, ID: The Caxton Printers, Ltd., 1949.

An abridged version of *Adventures on the Columbia River* by Ross Cox and *Fur Hunters in the Far West* by Alexander Ross, both published in the nineteenth century and long out of print. See individual entries for information on these two titles.

Ewers, John C. *Early White Influence Upon Plains Indian Painting: George Catlin and Carl Bodmer Among the Mandan, 1832–1834.* Washington, D. C.: Smithsonian Institution, 1957. Reprinted in 1988 by Territorial Press.

An interesting overview of the effects that Catlin and Bodmer had upon the Plains Indians during the two artists' travels among them in the early 1830s.

————— , Gallagher, Marsha V., Hunt, David C., and Porter, Joseph C. *Views of a Vanishing Frontier.* Omaha: Center for Western Studies/Joslyn Art Museum, 1984.

An attractive catalog that depicts an exhibition of Karl Bodmer's paintings at the Joslyn Art Museum in Omaha, Nebraska. The informative text places Bodmer and his sponsor, Prince Maximilian, in the proper perspective against the backdrop of the 1830s Rocky Mountain fur trade.

Favour, Alpheus H. *Old Bill Williams, Mountain Man.* Norman: University of Oklahoma Press, 1962.

A well-done biography of Williams, one of the better known mountain men.

Ferris, Warren Angus. *Life in the Rocky Mountains.* Salt Lake City: Rocky Mountain Book Shop, 1940.

The previously unpublished journal of mountain man Warren Ferris, during his stay in the Rockies from 1830 until 1835. The book gives the first full-length description of the Yellowstone region. Another edition of Ferris's book was published by The Old West Publishing Company in Denver at about the same time.

Fisher, Vardis. *Mountain Man.* New York: 1965. Reprinted in 1967 and several times since by Pocket Books.

Although a work of fiction, this book, like A. B. Guthrie's novels, is must reading for the fur trade aficionado. Fisher does a masterful job at portraying the life of a mountain man. His main character is loosely based on the life of "Liver Eating" Johnston. The movie, *Jeremiah Johnson,* was partially adapted from this book.

Franchere, Gabriel. *Adventure at Astoria 1810–1814.* Norman: University of Oklahoma Press, 1967.
    The adventures of a young Frenchman who helped establish Astoria as part of John J. Astor's northwestern fur empire.

Garrard, Lewis Hector. *Wah-To-Yah, and the Taos Trail.* Cincinnati: H. W. Derby & Co., 1850. Reprinted in 1955 by the University of Oklahoma Press.
    Described by A. B. Guthrie, Jr. as "the genuine article—the Indian, the trader, the mountain man, their dress, and behavior and speech and the country and climate they lived in," this book is essential to the fur trade enthusiast. Garrard provided the only eye-witness account of the Taos trials that convicted the killers of fur trader Charles Bent.

Ghent, W. J. *The Early Far West: A Narrative Outline, 1540–1850.* New York: Longmans, Green and Co., 1931. Reprinted in 1936 by Tudor Publishing Co.
    In this book, according to the author's own words, "especial attention is given to the movements of the fur-trappers, for these heroic men were true explorers who opened to the knowledge of the world a vast region." The book quite nicely covers the rise and fall of the western fur trade.

Gilbert, Bil. *The Trailblazers.* Alexandria, VA: Time-Life Books, 1973.
    Part of the extremely well-done Time-Life "The Old West" series, this volume covers the mountain man era and the personalities who participated in it.

_____. *Westering Man: The Life of Joseph Walker*. New York: Atheneum, 1983.

An in-depth biography of the Tennessee-born mountain man who helped survey the Santa Fe Trail and who became the first white man to see Yosemite.

Goetzmann, William H. *Exploration and Empire: The Explorer and the Scientist in the Winning of the American West*. New York: Alfred A. Knopf, 1966. Reprinted in 1993 by the Texas State Historical Association.

Goetzmann, who is one of the nation's foremost western historians, won the 1967 Pulitzer Prize in history for this book. It contains a well-done chapter on "The Mountain Men."

_____. *New Lands, New Men: America and the Second Great Age of Discovery*. New York: Viking Penguin, Inc., 1986. Reprinted in 1995 by the Texas State Historical Association.

This book takes a look at the American mountain man as a primary factor in the early exploration of the West. It reaffirms most modern-day fur-trade historians' feelings that members of the fur trading/trapping community were, indeed, responsible for the first and most complete exploration of the trans-Mississippi region.

_____; Hunt, David C.; Gallagher, Marsha V.; and Orr, William J. *Karl Bodmer's America*. Lincoln: University of Nebraska Press, 1984.

A magnificent book that reproduces in full color, as well as in black and white, most of Bodmer's art produced on his trip up the Missouri River with Prince Maximilian in the years 1832 to 1834. It includes a comprehensive biography of Bodmer.

_____ and Williams, Glyndwr. *The Atlas of North American Exploration*. New York: Prentice Hall General Reference, 1992.

A wonderful collection of full-color maps, along with accompanying explanations, that depict all facets of New World exploration, from the Norse voyages in 1,000 A.D. to the races for the North and South Poles. Includes several excellent maps pertaining to the western fur trade.

Gowans, Fred R. *Rocky Mountain Rendezvous: A History of the Fur Trade Rendezvous 1825–1840.* Provo, UT: Brigham Young University, 1976. Reprinted in 1985 by Peregrine Smith Books.

An interesting book that identifies and illustrates each of the Rocky Mountain rendezvous sites and documents the primary events of each get-together.

Grant, Bruce. *American Forts Yesterday and Today.* New York: E. P. Dutton & Co., 1965.

A good, readable "guidebook" to American forts and their histories, including many installations that were built primarily as fur posts.

Guthrie, A. B., Jr. *The Big Sky.* New York: William Sloane Associates, 1947. Reprinted many times.

This book is fictional, but, perhaps more than any other novel, it captures the spirit of the mountain man era. Follows the adventures of Boone Caudill from his birthplace in Kentucky to the Shinin' Mountains and home again. It contains vivid descriptions of the mountains and the trying events that Caudill faced in his quest to be a mountain man. Guthrie was a master storyteller.

_____ . *The Way West.* New York: William Sloane Associates, 1949. Reprinted many times.

The winner of the 1950 Pulitzer Prize for fiction, this book picks up the adventures of Boone Caudill where *The Big Sky* leaves off. An outstanding "Mountain Man" novel.

Hafen, LeRoy R. *Broken Hand: The Life of Thomas Fitzpatrick: Mountain Man, Guide and Indian Agent.* Denver: Old West Publishing Co., 1973. Reprinted in 1981 by the University of Nebraska Press.

A well-executed biography about Fitzpatrick, written by one of America's premier historians. The late LeRoy R. Hafen was a prolific writer, whose body of work included many classics about the West, not the least of which is this volume.

_____ and W. J. Ghent. *Broken Hand: The Life Story of Thomas Fitzpatrick, Chief of the Mountain Men.* Denver: 1931.

An older biography of Fitzpatrick which has largely been superseded by the previous entry by Leroy Hafen.

_____ and Francis M. Young. *Fort Laramie and the Pageant of the West, 1834–1890.* Glendale: The Arthur H. Clark Company, 1938. Reprinted in 1984 by the University of Nebraska Press.

This is probably the best book ever written about the history of Fort Laramie, from its early fur trade days till to its final demise as a United States army post.

_____ , Editor. Selected and with an introduction by Janet Lecompte. *French Fur Traders and Voyageurs in the American West.* Spokane, WA: The Arthur H. Clark Company, 1995. Reprinted in 1997 by the University of Nebraska Press.

A selection of biographical sketches of twenty-five French mountain men, extracted from Hafen's monumental set, *The Mountain Men and the Fur Trade of the Far West.*

_____ , Editor. *Fur Traders, Trappers, and Mountain Men of the Upper Missouri.* Lincoln: University of Nebraska Press, 1995.

The lives of eighteen mountain men employed by the American Fur Company and its successors are featured in

154

this selection from Hafen's *The Mountain Men and the Fur Trade of the Far West.*

_____ , Editor. Selected and with an introduction by Harvey L. Carter. *Mountain Men and Fur Traders of the Far West.* Lincoln: University of Nebraska Press, 1982.

A careful selection of sketches about eighteen prominent figures in the Western fur trade, taken from Hafen's ten volume set, *The Mountain Men and the Fur Trade of the Far West.* Included in this volume are Manuel Lisa, Pierre Chouteau, Jr., Wilson Price Hunt, William H. Ashley, Jedediah Smith, John McLoughlin, Peter Skene Ogden, Ceran St. Vrain, Kit Carson, "Old Bill" Williams, William Sublette, Thomas Fitzpatrick, James Bridger, Benjamin L. E. Bonneville, Joseph R. Walker, Nathaniel Wyeth, Andrew Drips, and Joe Meek.

_____ , Editor. *The Mountain Men and the Fur Trade of the Far West.* Glendale: The Arthur H. Clark Company, 1965–72.

A ten volume set of encyclopedic proportions that chronicles the lives of 292 mountain men and fur company officials, each one written by an authority in his or her field. The complete set has long been out-of-print and commands a premium price in the rare book market. Although this set is usually found only in larger libraries, selected biographies from it have been published in various, still-available collections. See above and below entries.

_____ , Editor. Selected and with an introduction by Harvey L. Carter. *Trappers of the Far West.* Lincoln: University of Nebraska Press, 1983.

Sixteen additional biographical selections from Hafen's *Mountain Men and the Fur Trade of the Far West,* including Etienne Provost, James Ohio Pattie, Louis Robidoux, Ewing Young, David E. Jackson, Milton Sublette, Lucien Fontenelle, James Clyman, James P. Beckwourth, Edward and Francis Ermatinger, John Gantt,

William Bent, Charles Autobees, Warren Angus Ferris, Manuel Alvarez, and Robert Campbell.

_____ , Editor. *With Fur Traders in Colorado, 1839–40: The Journal of E. Willard Smith.* Franklin: TN: Territorial Press, 1988.

Preserves E. Willard Smith's journal, "one of the best records of conditions and activity in the Colorado region during fur trade days." Smith was given the trip West as a graduation present, and he spent nearly two years "roughing it" with the mountain men of the Rocky Mountains.

Harris, Burton. *John Colter: His Years in the Rockies.* New York: Charles Scribners & Sons, 1952. Reprinted in 1983 by Big Horn Book Company and in 1993 by the University of Nebraska Press.

The only book-length biography of the Virginian who left the Lewis and Clark Expedition on its way home and headed back for the Rockies, thus becoming the "first" mountain man and the first white man to view the wonders of present-day Yellowstone National Park.

Hassrick, Royal B. *The George Catlin Book of American Indians.* New York: Watson-Guptill Publications, 1977. Reprinted in 1981 by Promontory Press.

A collection of color and black and white reproductions of some of Catlin's outstanding paintings of trans-Mississippi Indian tribes during his visits among them during the early 1830s.

Hawgood, John A. *America's Western Frontiers: The Exploration and Settlement of the Trans-Mississippi West.* New York: Alfred A Knopf, 1967.

The first winner of the Alfred A. Knopf Western History Prize. Contains an interesting chapter entitled, "Fur Traders and Trappers of the Far West."

Hoig, Stan. *The Western Odyssey of John Simpson Smith, Trapper, Trader and Interpreter.* Glendale: The Arthur H. Clark Company, 1974.

The story of a little-known, yet important, mountain man. Smith was active as a trader/trapper during the mid-1840s when he frequented Fort Laramie and Bent's Fort. He later became an interpreter and guide and was a founder of Denver.

Holmes, Kenneth L. *Ewing Young: Master Trapper.* Portland, OR: Binfords & Mort, Publishers, 1967.

The only book-length biography available about the Tennessee-born mountain man who was active in both the Southwest and Northwest fur trade for many years.

Hyde, George E. *A Life of George Bent Written From His Letters.* Norman: University of Oklahoma Press, 1968.

Although George Bent—the son of Bent's Fort builder, William, and his Cheyenne wife, Owl Woman—was not born until 1843, this book has value for the fur trade student. Based on Bent's letters to the author, dating from 1905 until his death in 1918, it reveals interesting, firsthand information about Bent's Fort during its declining years.

Into the Wilderness. Washington: D. C.: National Geographic Society, 1978.

The chapter written by Michael W. Robbins and entitled, "A Reckless Breed," depicts the trial and tribulations of the mountain men.

Irving, Washington. *Astoria, or Anecdotes of an Enterprise Beyond the Rocky Mountains.* Philadelphia: Carey, Lea, & Blanchard, 1836. Reprinted many times.

    After all these years, Irving's study of John Jacob Astor's northwestern fur empire remains one of the best. Written by one of America's foremost authors of the time, the book benefits from Irving's ability to gather first-hand accounts of the enterprise.

ASTORIA,

OR

ANECDOTES OF AN ENTERPRISE

BEYOND THE

ROCKY MOUNTAINS.

BY WASHINGTON IRVING.

IN TWO VOLUMES.
VOL. I.

PHILADELPHIA:
CAREY, LEA, & BLANCHARD.
1836.

_____ . *Adventures of Captain Bonneville, or Scenes Beyond the Rocky Mountains of the Far West.* London: Richard Bentley, 1837. Reprinted many times, including an undated, probably 1960s edition, by Binfords & Mort, Portland, OR.

    Covers the adventures of French-born Benjamin Louis Eulalie Bonneville, a West Point graduate who, in 1832, took a three-year leave of absence from his army duties to try his hand at the Rocky Mountain fur trade.

Isely, Bliss. *Blazing the Way West.* New York, 1939.

    A popularized account of the western fur trade from the days of early French influence to the establishment of the Bent, St. Vrain Company in the early 1830s.

Jablow, Joseph. *The Cheyenne in Plains Indian Trade Relations, 1795–1840.* New York: J. J. Augustin, 1951. Reprinted in 1995 by University of Nebraska Press.

A very interesting book that explores Plains Indian trading patterns and tribal relationships with American fur traders and trappers.

Jackson, Donald. *Thomas Jefferson & the Stony Mountains: Exploring the West from Monticello.* Urbana: University of Illinois Press, 1981.
An interesting account of Thomas Jefferson's role in shaping the exploration of the trans-Mississippi West. At the time of his death in 1987, Donald Jackson was America's foremost authority on Lewis and Clark and the Expedition.

———— . *Voyages of the Steamboat Yellowstone.* New York: Ticknor & Fields, 1985.
A short history of the famous steamboat owned by John Jacob Astor's American Fur Company and which carried such dignitaries as George Catlin, Karl Bodmer, and the war chief, Black Hawk, upon its decks.

Jackson, John C. *Shadow on the Tetons: David E. Jackson and the Claiming of the American West.* Missoula, MT: Mountain Press Publishing Company, 1993.
A very well done biography of the man after whom Jackson Hole, Wyoming was named. Sometimes overshadowed by more popularized individuals such as Jedediah Smith, William H. Ashley, and the Sublette brothers, Jackson was, nevertheless, an important figure in the Rocky Mountain fur trade.

James, Thomas. *Three Years Among the Indians and Mexicans.* Waterloo, IL: Printed at the Office of the "War Eagle," 1846. Reprinted in 1966 by The Citadel Press.

THREE YEARS AMONG

THE

INDIANS AND MEXICANS.

BY GEN. THOMAS JAMES,
OF MONROE COUNTY, ILLINOIS.

WATERLOO, ILL.
PRINTED AT THE OFFICE OF THE "WAR EAGLE."
1846.

This is the journal of one of the first Americans to travel along the upper Missouri River. James was an employee of Manuel Lisa's Missouri Fur Company and during the first upstream expedition of 1809–10, he left a good insight into what the region was like in those early fur-trade days.

Kelly, Charles. *Old Greenwood: The Story of Caleb Greenwood, Trapper, Pathfinder and Early Pioneer of the West.* Salt Lake City, 1936.

Greenwood was an early trapper who arrived in St. Louis as early as 1808. He traveled part of the way to the Pacific with the Overland Astorians, then went to work for Manuel Lisa. As a free trapper, he ranged the mountains from the upper Arkansas to present-day Montana. This is his story.

_____ and Dale Morgan. *Old Greenwood.* Georgetown, CA, 1965.

A revised and greatly enlarged version of the previous title.

Kurz, Rudolph Friederich. *Journal of Rudolph Friederich Kurz: An Account of His Experiences among Fur Traders and American Indians on the Mississippi and the Upper Missouri Rivers during the Years 1846 to 1852.* Washington, D. C.: Bureau of American Ethnology, 1937.

A fully illustrated account of this young Swiss artist's journey to the American West. The hundreds of sketches made during his travels, plus his diary entries, are of primary importance in the documentation of the period.

Lamar, Howard, R., Editor. *The Reader's Encyclopedia of the American West.* New York: Harper & Row, Publishers, 1977.

An essential reference for the student of the American West. Contains numerous entries and articles pertaining to the western fur trade.

Larpenteur, Charles. *Forty Years as a Fur Trader on the Upper Missouri: The Personal Narrative of Charles Larpenteur, 1833–1872.* New York, 1898. Reprinted in 1989 by the University of Nebraska Press.

Called by one authority "a remarkable document on the American fur trade," Larpenteur's book describes his many years as a free trapper and as an employee of the American Fur Company. Contains a graphic account of the smallpox epidemic of 1837.

Lavender, David. *Bent's Fort.* Garden City, NY: Doubleday & Company, 1954. Reprinted in 1972 by the University of Nebraska Press.

Provides the complete story of the Bent, St. Vrain Company and its Colorado headquarters, Bent's Fort. Written by one of the true "masters" of western history, the book was the winner of the Western Writers of America's first Spur Award for nonfiction.

_____ . *Fort Laramie and the Changing Frontier*. Washington, D. C.: National Park Service, 1983.

A well-done guide to Fort Laramie. Although it ended its long career as a U.S. Cavalry installation, Fort Laramie started out as a privately-owned fur post. This volume is the official National Park "handbook" with lots of color and black and white illustrations.

_____ . *The Fist in the Wilderness*. Garden City, NY: Doubleday & Company, 1964.

Lavender provides an in-depth look at John Jacob Astor's American Fur Company and the men who managed it, told from the viewpoint of one of the company's most influential members, Ramsey Crooks.

Laycock, George. *The Mountain Men*. Danbury, CT: Outdoor Life Books, 1988.

A nice, well-illustrated book that gives a good overview of the life, times, equipment, and prey of the mountain man.

Legg, John. *Shinin' Trails: A Possibles Bag of Fur Trade Trivia*. Ogden, UT: Eagle's View Publishing Company, 1988.

A neat little book that will keep you entertained for hours. Contains hundreds of questions and answers about every aspect of the fur trade.

Leonard, Zenas. *Adventures of a Mountain Man: The Narrative of Zenas Leonard*. Lincoln: University of Nebraska Press, 1978.

The personal narrative of the adventures of a mountain man who accompanied Joseph Walker across the Sierra Nevadas to California to become one of the first white men to view Yosemite. Called by one authority as "the most complete and accurate account" of the Walker expedition.

Le Roy, Bruce, Editor. *H. M. Chittenden: A Western Epic.*
Tacoma: Washington State Historical Society, 1961.
An excellent introductory study of the man who is universally recognized as the "father" of western fur trade literature. Contains a selection from his unpublished journals, diaries, and reports.

Luttig, John C. *Journal of a Fur-Trading Expedition On the
Upper Missouri 1812–1813.* New York: Argosy-Antiquarian
Ltd., 1964.
Reproduces the only known personal journal of the
very early days of the Missouri and Rocky Mountain fur
trade. Luttig was a clerk for Manuel Lisa's Missouri Fur
Company. An appendix contains a copy of the original arti-
cles of Missouri Fur's incorporation in 1812.

McCracken, Harold. *George Catlin and the Old Frontier.* New
York: Dial Press, 1959. Reprinted several times by
Bonanza Books.
A well-done biography of Catlin, written by one of
America's foremost Western art historians.

McDermott, John Francis, Editor. *Travelers on the Western
Frontier.* Urbana: University of Illinois Press, 1970.
A fascinating book composed of essays by well-known
Western historians about historical source material and
where to find it. Contains a great deal about the fur trade.

Maloney, Alice Bay, Editor. *Fur Brigade to the Bonaventura.
John Work's California Expedition 1832–1833 for the
Hudson's Bay Co.* San Francisco: 1945.
Documents Work's mission to California for the
Hudson's Bay Company in 1832 at which time he made con-
tact with both Spanish and Russian authorities. In 1846,
Work succeeded John McLoughlin as the Hudson's Bay
chief factor at Fort Vancouver.

Manfred, Frederick. *Lord Grizzly.* Lincoln: University of Nebraska Press, 1983.

A highly readable, fictionalized account of Hugh Glass's ordeal with the grizzly bear.

Mattes, Merrill J. *Colter's Hell & Jackson's Hole.* Yellowstone Library and Museum Association, 1962.

Reveals the complete story of John Colter's exploration of the Yellowstone and Grand Teton regions, along with valuable background information about the Rocky Mountain fur trade in general.

Maximilian, Prince Alexander Philip. *Travels in the Interior of North America in the Years 1832, 1833, and 1834.* Cleveland: The Arthur H. Clark Company, 1906.

The journals of Prince Maximilian who, with his Swiss-born artist, Karl Bodmer, traveled on the upper Missouri River among the fur traders in the early 1830s.

Meriwether, David. *My Life in the Mountains and on the Plains.* Norman: University of Oklahoma Press, 1965.

The autobiography of an early governor of New Mexico Territory who, as a young man, lived the life of a mountain man and fur trader on the upper Missouri River and in New Mexico.

Mirsky, Jeannette. *The Westward Crossings.* New York: Alfred A. Knopf, 1946.

Part II of this book gives an interesting account of the early French, British, and Russian fur trade in the far Northwest before Lewis and Clark.

Morgan, Dale L. *Jedediah Smith and the Opening of the West.* Indianapolis: The Bobbs-Merrill Company, Inc., 1953. Reprinted in 1964 by the University of Nebraska Press.

Far more than a biography of Jedediah Smith, this book, written by a master historian and an authority on the

Rocky Mountain fur trade, delves into the complete history of the William Ashley-Andrew Henry relationship; the rendezvous system; the Smith Jackson & Sublette Company, and the later Rocky Mountain Fur Company. A "must-have" volume for any fur-trade library.

_____ and Eleanor Towles Harris, Editors. *The Rocky Mountain Journals of William Marshall Anderson: The West in 1834.* San Marino, CA: The Ward Ritchie Press, 1967. Reprinted in 1987 by the University of Nebraska Press.

  This interesting volume documents the western travels of Anderson, a first cousin of Chief Justice John Marshall, during the year 1834. Robert Glass Cleland, author of *This Reckless Breed of Men,* called Anderson's journals "of very great importance, not only because of its account of fur trading, but also because of its contribution to the whole history of the opening of the West."

_____ ., Editor. *The West of William H. Ashley.* Denver: The Old West Publishing Company, 1964.

  An over-sized, stunningly beautiful book that unfortunately has been long out-of-print. Morgan presents letters and records from first-hand diaries that depict the struggle for the western fur trade.

Mumey, Nolie. *Old Forts and Trading Posts of the West: Bent's Old Fort and Bent's New Fort on the Arkansas River.* Denver: Artcraft Press, 1956.

  A definitive study of the two forts belonging to the noted fur-trading Bent family. Contains much original documentation and many letters and other items of correspondence from the period.

Myers, John Myers. *The Deaths of the Bravos.* Boston: Little, Brown & Company, 1962. Reprinted in 1995 as *Bravos of the West* by the University of Nebraska Press.

A collection of interesting stories about many characters of the Old West, including several mountain men and fur traders.

_____ . *The Saga of Hugh Glass: Pirate, Pawnee, and Mountain Man.* Boston: Little, Brown and Company, 1963. Reprinted in 1976 by the University of Nebraska Press.

The biography of Hugh Glass, the indomitable mountain man who is best remembered for his struggle with the grizzly bear and his hair-raising ordeal after he was left for dead in the wilderness by his companions.

Nasatir, A. P., Editor. *Before Lewis and Clark.* St. Louis: St. Louis Historical Documents Foundation, 1952. Reprinted in 1990 by the University of Nebraska Press.

An important two-volume work that deals primarily with Spanish and French exploration and trade relations in the Missouri River Valley prior to 1800. Contains original documents relating to the era. This book is essential to those interested in the period of pre-American contact in the Missouri Valley.

National Park Service. *Soldier and Brave.* New York: Harper & Row, Publishers, 1963.

Volume XII of the National Survey of Historic Sites and Buildings, this book's primary subject is military forts and installations. However, some references are made to fur posts, such as Bent's Fort, Fort Union, and Fort Vancouver.

Newman, Peter C. *Caesars of the Wilderness.* Ontario: Penguin Books, 1987.

Book Two of a three volume series by an authority on the Hudson's Bay Company. Although its theater of operations was primarily in Canada, Hudson's Bay did reach southward into the Pacific Northwest in the present-day United States. Operating out of Fort Vancouver on the

Columbia River, HBC was an important competitor in the trans-Mississippi trade for several years.

_____ . *Company of Adventurers.* Ontario: Penguin Books, 1985.
Book One of the above series about the Hudson's Bay Company. Covers the very early days of HBC.

_____ . *Empire on the Bay: An Illustrated History of the Hudson's Bay Company.* Ontario: Penguin Books, 1989.
As the title indicates, this book is a pictorial history of HBC, with some reference to American operations. Lavishly illustrated in full-color.

Nitske, W. Robert, Translator, and Savoie Lottinville, Editor. *Paul Wilhelm, Duke of Wurttemberg: Travels in North America 1822–1824.* Norman: University of Oklahoma Press, 1973.
Documents this German nobleman's 1823 excursion up the Missouri River with fur traders as far as the White River.

Ogden, Peter Skene. *Traits of American Indian Life and Character.* London: Smith, Elder and Company, 1853. Reprinted in 1995 by Dover Publications, Inc.
Written by the famed Canadian-born fur man, the book is primarily a narrative of Ogden's fur trading/trapping career with the Hudson's Bay Company in Oregon.

Oglesby, Richard. *Manuel Lisa and the Opening of the Missouri Fur Trade.* Norman: University of Oklahoma Press, 1963.
An outstanding biography of the man who founded the Missouri Fur Company and who was the first to launch a serious American effort at trading with the Indians of the Missouri River basin. One of the "must-have" volumes in any fur trade library.

O'Neal, Bill. *Fighting Men of the Indian Wars.* Stillwater, OK: Barbed Wire Press, 1991.

A collection of brief biographies about Westerners, including a few of the better-known mountain men (Jim Bridger, John Colter, Milton Sublette, Ewing Young, and others).

Pattie, James Ohio. *The Personal Narrative of James O. Pattie, of Kentucky.* Cincinnati: John H. Wood, 1831. Reprinted in 1962 by J. B. Lippincott Company.

Pattie's first-hand account of his 1824–27 travels in present-day New Mexico, Arizona, California, and Mexico as a fur trapper and trader.

THE

PERSONAL NARRATIVE

OF

JAMES O. PATTIE,

OF

KENTUCKY,

DURING AN EXPEDITION FROM ST. LOUIS, THROUGH THE VAST REGIONS BETWEEN THAT PLACE AND THE PACIFIC OCEAN, AND THENCE BACK THROUGH THE CITY OF MEXICO TO VERA CRUZ, DURING JOURNEY-INGS OF SIX YEARS; IN WHICH HE AND HIS FATHER, WHO ACCOMPANIED HIM, SUFFERED UNHEARD OF HARDSHIPS AND DANGERS, HAD VARIOUS CONFLICTS WITH THE IN-DIANS, AND WERE MADE CAPTIVES, IN WHICH CAPTIVITY HIS FATHER DIED; TOGETHER WITH A DESCRIPTION OF THE COUNTRY, AND THE VARIOUS NATIONS THROUGH WHICH THEY PASSED.

EDITED BY TIMOTHY FLINT.

CINCINNATI:
PRINTED AND PUBLISHED BY JOHN H. WOOD.
1831.

Pearsall, Clarence E.; Murray, George D.; Tibbetts, A. C.; Neall, Harry L.; and Lewis, Oscar, Editors. *The Quest for Qual-A-Wa-Loo.* San Francisco: 1943.

A compilation of information from various sources relating to the exploration of northern California, including an 1828 journal by Harrison G. Rogers, one of Jedediah Smith's companions during the famed mountain man's California years.

Phillips, Paul Chrisler. *The Fur Trade.* Norman: University of Oklahoma Press, 1961.

A magisterial, two-volume work that covers all facets

of the American fur trade. Much of Volume Two relates specifically to the western trade. Unfortunately, at the time of this writing, this classic has been out of print for a number of years.

Porter, Mae Reed and Davenport, Odessa. *Scotsman in Buckskin: Sir William Drummond Stewart and the Rocky Mountain Fur Trade.* New York: Hastings House, Publishers, 1963.

A fine biography of the Scots nobleman who traveled to the American West during the mid 1830s to become a mountain man.

Ronda, James. *Astoria and Empire.* Lincoln: University of Nebraska Press, 1990.

The fascinating story of John Jacob Astor's fur-trading empire in the Pacific Northwest, with headquarters at the mouth of the Columbia River.

Ross, Alexander. *Adventures of the First Settlers on the Oregon or Columbia River: Being a Narrative of the Expedition Fitted Out by John Jacob Astor, to Establish The "Pacific Fur Company;" With an Account of Some Indian Tribes on the Coast of the Pacific.* London: Smith, Elder & Co., 1849. Reprinted in 1923 as a Lakeside Classic.

An essential book for the student of John Jacob Astor's Northwest fur empire and its headquarters at Astoria. Presents a dramatic account of one man's experience with the company and his observations of its daily operations, as well as interesting insights into neighboring Indian tribes.

Ross, Marvin C. *The West of Alfred Jacob Miller.* Norman: University of Oklahoma Press, 1951.

A fascinating collection of the art work and on-site notes of Alfred Jacob Miller, the Baltimore painter who accompanied Captain William Drummond Stewart to the wilds of the American West in 1837. Miller's paintings are the only visual eye-witness accounts of the waning days of the Rocky Mountain fur trade period.

Russell, Carl P. *Guns on the Early Frontiers.* Berkeley: University of California Press, 1957. Reprinted several times, most recently by Barnes & Noble.

An excellent introduction into the wide variety of firearms that was used in early America, including the fur trade period. An excellent reference guide.

_____. *Firearms, Traps, & Tools of the Mountain Men.* New York: Alfred A. Knopf, 1967. Reprinted by the University of New Mexico Press.

Provides a complete guide in picture and text to the mountain man's equipment during the 1820–40s period. This book is one of the "must" volumes for students of the fur trade.

Russell, Osborne. *Journal of a Trapper.* Lincoln: University of Nebraska Press, 1965. Reprinted in 1996 by MJF Books.

Called by one authority as "perhaps the finest record of mountain man life and adventures extant," Russell's book documents his early wanderings throughout the West as an employee of Nathaniel J. Wyeth, of the Rocky Mountain Fur Company, and as a free trapper.

Ruxton, George Frederick. *Life in the Far West.* New York: Harper & Brothers, Publishers, 1849. Reprinted in 1951 by the University of Oklahoma Press, with notes by LeRoy R. Hafen and illustrations by Alfred Jacob Miller.

Although fictionalized, this book has been described as a "fur trade . . . classic," based on solid historical fact. Ruxton, a young Englishman, traveled throughout the Rocky Mountain West during the mid 1840s, and this book is an accurate portrayal of what it was really like to be a mountain man.

Sandoz, Mari. *The Beaver Men: Spearheads of Empire.* New York: Hastings House, Publishers, 1964. Reprinted in 1978 by the University of Nebraska Press.
A very informative book that covers the western fur trade from the French and English days down through the formation of the Rocky Mountain Fur Company.

Satterfield, Archie and Lavender, David. *Fort Vancouver.* Washington, D. C.: National Park Service, 1981.
A history of the most noted fur post in the Pacific Northwest, the people who managed it, and its impact on the western fur trade. Well illustrated with color photos and art work.

Smith, Arthur D. Howden. *John Jacob Astor: Landlord of New York.* Philadelphia: J. B. Lippincott Company, 1929.
An older, somewhat outdated—but still useable—biography of the founder of the American Fur Company.

Spaulding, Kenneth, Editor. *On the Oregon Trail. Robert Stuart's Journey of Discovery (1812–1813).* Norman: University of Oklahoma Press, 1953. Also, the version with Philip Ashton Rollins as editor was published in 1995 by the University of Nebraska Press.
Documents the eastward-bound journey of Stuart, an employee of John Jacob Astor, from Astoria to St. Louis, during which time South Pass and the future path of the Oregon Trail were discovered.

Speck, Gordon. *Breeds and Half-Breeds.* New York: Clarkson N. Potter, Inc./Publisher, 1969.
Surveys the lives and careers of several fur trade personalities, including mountain men Jim Beckwourth and Edward Rose, along with George Drouillard and Pierre Dorion, Sr.

_____ . *Northwest Explorations.* Portland, OR: Binfords & Mort, Publishers, 1954.

An interesting appraisal of early Pacific Northwest exploration and explorers. The second half of the book contains much information on the fur trade, the North West Company, Manuel Lisa, John McLoughlin, and more.

Still, Bayrd, Editor. *The West: Contemporary Records of America's Expansion Across the Continent: 1607–1890.* New York: Capricorn Books, 1961.

This book provides first hand narratives from America's exploration and settlement periods. Part VI is entitled "Across the Wide Missouri" and contains some fur trade and mountain man material.

Story of the Great American West. Pleasantville, NY: The Reader's Digest Association, Inc., 1977.

A well-illustrated, generalized introduction to the history of the West, containing a chapter on the mountain men.

Sullivan, Maurice S. *The Travels of Jedediah Smith.* Santa Ana, CA: Fine Arts Press, 1934. Reprinted in 1992 by the University of Nebraska Press.

Covers practically all of Smith's remarkable fur trade career, from his first employment with General William Ashley in 1822 to his crossing of the Utah desert on his way to California in 1828. Includes Smith's own diary of these years.

Sunder, John E. *Bill Sublette: Mountain Man.* Norman: University of Oklahoma Press, 1959.

A well-done biography of William Sublette, one of five Kentucky brothers—and the most successful—all active in the western fur trade. Sublette was instrumental in breaking John Jacob Astor's monopoly on the upper Missouri trade.

_____ . *Joshua Pilcher: Fur Trader and Indian Agent.* Norman: University of Oklahoma Press, 1968.

The definitive biography of Pilcher, the Missouri Fur Company's number-two man who took over the organization's operations when Manuel Lisa died in 1820.

Thomas, Davis and Ronnefeldt, Karin, Editors. *People of the First Man: Life Among the Plains Indians in Their Final Days of Glory.* New York: Promontory Press, 1982.

A beautifully executed abridgment of Prince Maximilian's journal documenting his five thousand mile trip with his artist-companion, Karl Bodmer, along the Missouri River in 1833–34. Guests of the American Fur Company, the pair of travelers witnessed some of the glory days of the Rocky Mountain fur trade.

Thompson, Erwin N. *Fort Union Trading Post: Fur Trade Empire on the Upper Missouri.* Medora, ND: Theodore Roosevelt Nature and History Association, 1986.

Traces the history of Fort Union on the upper Missouri, from its founding by Kenneth McKenzie in 1829 as one of the most important fur posts in the northern Great Plains, until its purchase by the United States government in 1867.

Thorp, Raymond W. and Bunker, Robert. *Crow Killer: The Saga of Liver-Eating Johnson.* Bloomington, IN: Indiana University Press, 1958.

An interesting biography of John Johnson, or Johnston, one of the few mountain men who survived into the twentieth century. He claimed to have killed three hundred Crow warriors, whose kinsmen had earlier murdered his wife. The movie, *Jeremiah Johnson,* was partially based on this book.

Thrapp, Dan L. *Encyclopedia of Frontier Biography.* Glendale, CA: The Arthur H. Clark Company, 1988. Reprinted in 1991 by the University of Nebraska Press.

A massive three-volume collection of biographies of hundreds of frontier figures, including the more important mountain men and players in the western fur trade.

_____ . *Encyclopedia of Frontier Biography, Volume Four.* Spokane, WA: The Arthur H. Clark Company, 1994.

A supplement to the above three-volume series. Contains a few more fur trade-related entries. Not available as a reprint.

Vestal, Stanley. *Jim Bridger: Mountain Man.* New York: William Morrow & Company, 1946. Reprinted in 1970 by the University of Nebraska Press.

Somewhat dated, but still a valuable biography of one of the most recognized names in western fur trade history, written by a noted Western historian.

_____ . *Joe Meek: The Merry Mountain Man.* Caldwell, ID: Caxton Printers, Ltd., 1952. Reprinted in 1963 by the University of Nebraska Press.

A well-done biography of mountain man and Oregon pioneer, Joe Meek.

Victor, Frances Fuller. *The River of the West. Life and Adventure in the Rocky Mountains and Oregon, etc.* Hartford, CT: R. W. Bliss & Company, 1870. Reprinted in 1983 and 1985 as *The River of the West: The Adventures of Joe Meek,* in two volumes by Mountain Press Publishing Company of Missoula, MT.

Covers the life and career of Meek, one of the more eminent mountain men, from his fur trade days to his retirement in Oregon where he helped organize the territory and served in a number of civil positions.

THE RIVER OF THE WEST.

LIFE AND ADVENTURE
IN THE

ROCKY MOUNTAINS AND OREGON;
EMBRACING EVENTS IN THE LIFE-TIME OF A

MOUNTAIN-MAN AND PIONEER:
WITH THE

EARLY HISTORY OF THE NORTH-WESTERN SLOPE,
INCLUDING

AN ACCOUNT OF THE FUR TRADERS, THE INDIAN TRIBES, THE OVERLAND IMMIGRA-
TION, THE OREGON MISSIONS, AND THE TRAGIC FATE OF
REV. DR. WHITMAN AND FAMILY.

ALSO, A DESCRIPTION OF THE COUNTRY,

ITS CONDITION, PROSPECTS, AND RESOURCES; ITS SOIL, CLIMATE, AND SCENERY;
ITS MOUNTAINS, RIVERS, VALLEYS, DESERTS, AND PLAINS; ITS
INLAND WATERS, AND NATURAL WONDERS.

WITH NUMEROUS ENGRAVINGS.

BY MRS. FRANCES FULLER VICTOR.

PUBLISHED BY SUBSCRIPTION ONLY.

Hartford, Conn., and Toledo, Ohio:
R. W. BLISS & COMPANY.
BLISS & COMPANY, NEWARK, N. J.
R. J. TRUMBULL & CO., SAN FRANCISCO, CAL.
1870.

Viola, Herman J. *Exploring the West.* Washington, D. C.: Smithsonian Institution, 1987.

A magnificent book, illustrated in full color, that depicts the early exploration and mapping of the American West. Contains an important chapter on Thomas Jefferson's dream of a western empire and the mountain men who followed Lewis and Clark.

Wagner, Henry R. and Camp, Charles L. Fourth Edition, Revised, Enlarged and Edited by Robert H. Becker. *The Plains & the Rockies: A Critical Bibliography of Exploration, Adventure and Travel in the American West 1800—1865.* San Francisco: John Howell-Books, 1982.

The absolute best source for early western fur trade titles and their authors. Contains references and lengthy descriptions of nearly five hundred rare books about the exploration and early settlement of the American West.

Weber David J. *The Californios versus Jedediah Smith 1826–1827*. Spokane, WA: The Arthur H. Clark Company, 1990.

Reproduces and analyzes a new cache of original documents relating to Jedediah Smith's sojourn in California.

_____ . *The Taos Trappers: The Fur Trade in the Far Southwest, 1540–1846*. Norman: University of Oklahoma Press, 1970.

The most recent of only two books that deal exclusively with the fur trade in the Southwest, the other one being Robert Glass Cleland's *This Reckless Breed of Men* (see above entry). Extremely well researched and written.

White, David A. *News of the Plains and Rockies 1803–1865*. Spokane, WA: The Arthur H. Clark Company, 1996.

The first of a projected eight volume series that will contain original narratives of overland travel and adventure from the Wagner-Camp and Becker bibliography of Western Americana. A good seventy-five per cent of this volume is dedicated to scarce fur trade narratives from 1813 until 1847.

Wilson, Iris H. *William Wolfskill, 1798–1866, Frontier Trapper to California Ranchero*. Glendale: The Arthur H. Clark Company, 1965.

The definitive biography of Kentucky-born mountain man, William Wolfskill, who was active in the New Mexican fur trade during the 1820s and who later settled in California and dramatically contributed to the economic development of the region.

Wishart, David J. *The Fur Trade of the American West, 1807–1840*. Lincoln: University of Nebraska Press, 1979.

A somewhat technical look at the physical, biological, and cultural environments of the western fur trade. This book surveys the strategies and annual cycles of operations of the trade.